7/6/97

Happy Lisa!
Birthday Lisa!
There is nothing
better than a good
travel escape in the
summer! Enjoy this
fun read.

Have a great trip to
Mexico and Portugal! :)
Love you lil!

Kim

A Cottage
in Portugal

· Richard Hewitt ·

Illustrations by
Barbara Finn Hewitt

SIMON & SCHUSTER
New York London Toronto Sydney Tokyo Singapore

SIMON & SCHUSTER
Rockefeller Center
1230 Avenue of the Americas
New York, NY 10020

Text copyright © 1996 by Richard Hewitt
Illustrations copyright © 1996 by Barbara Finn Hewitt

SIMON & SCHUSTER and colophon
are registered trademarks of Simon & Schuster Inc.

DESIGNED BY BARBARA MARKS

Manufactured in the United States of America

1 3 5 7 9 10 8 6 4 2

Library of Congress Cataloging-in-Publication Data
Hewitt, Richard.
A cottage in Portugal / Richard Hewitt ; illustrations by
Barbara Finn Hewitt.
p.   cm.
1. Hewitt, Richard. 2. Americans--Portugal--Biography.
3. Portugal--Biography.   I. Title.
CT1378.H48A3   1996
946.9'4200413'0092--dc20
[B]   95-40677
CIP

ISBN 0-684-81313-0

to Millie,
who was always there in time of need.

A Cottage
in Portugal

Sintra

1 IT WAS JUST AFTER CHRISTMAS when my wife Barbara and I drove across the Spanish frontier and entered Portugal. We expected perfect weather. Instead it was a dark, wet, and discouraging day, as we gradually descended the Portuguese plains heading toward the coast. A few hours later, on a radio full of static, we heard it announced that it was the heaviest rainfall on record in Portugal. We did not

doubt it. The newly constructed *autoestrada,* or highway, disappeared into the darkness ahead of us, submerged under a massive sheet of gray water. The pounding rain had completely obscured the demarcations on the fresh asphalt, and for some reason the highway lamps had not yet been connected to the electric grid. They stood, dark and sullen, at the road's edge.

Inside our recently acquired Volkswagen van, water leaked down through the sun roof, dripping onto the towels we had wrapped around our heads for protection. Behind us, in the rear of the van, wind and rain whistled through a window that had been broken during a robbery in France.

But if damp, we remained determined. For we were on our way to our new home, the home we planned to buy in Sintra.

We were not far from our destination. In fact, Sintra was only some 20 kilometers away. But still the gales of wind-driven rain continued, and to make matters worse, the van's heater was failing in its mission to defog the windshield. Barbara was wiping it with anything she could find that was still dry, including one of my T-shirts we had sacrificed to practicality. "Not a very auspicious beginning," she said.

And she was right. Robbed in Avignon and forced to spend countless days waiting for a consulate to process new passports, we had spent Christmas alone among strangers in the south of France. Things had not proceeded exactly as planned. We had sold our house in Massachusetts, packed up all the mementos of our past life and brought them with us on a freighter across the Atlantic. Was it too much to expect a bright welcome to our new home? After all, hadn't we chosen Portugal for its warm, sunny climate? Hadn't we left behind the snow and bitter temperatures of winter in New England, thrown away our mud boots and Pendletons forever? Yes, we had. We had also forgotten to pack umbrellas.

Barbara shouted a warning, and just in time I managed to pull the van off the highway into the breakdown lane as a massive, "articulated" semi-truck sped past, immersing us in dirty water. I hit the horn to object, but it shorted out after a brief toot and the truck disappeared into the thick, purple ink of the night. We must take more care, I thought. We had been warned that, statistically, Portuguese drivers were the worst in Europe. From what we had so far witnessed since crossing the border from Spain, it may have been an understatement. We had already passed any number of accidents: ruined vehicles in improbable positions surrounded by animated crowds of people, all probably proffering different versions of the cause. We had spent several minutes ourselves on each bizarre case, trying to imagine what particular violation of road ethics might have led to such contorted conclusions.

We stopped to examine our soaked map. Then, after wringing out the towels on our heads, we started up again and turned from the *autoestrada* onto a secondary road. It had less traffic, but it still kept me alert as I tried to negotiate a series of deep potholes. It was like driving on the moon. We lurched from one crater to the next, bouncing off our padded seats, grateful for our contrived headdresses that cushioned the blows when we ricocheted off the roof.

We found Sintra at last, more or less where we had left it the year before. But it looked somehow sadder under the cloak of rain and fog, even dismal perhaps. We briefly wondered if it could be the same magical, enchanted village we had come to know during a brief holiday, a village crowded with beautiful antiquities yet still parochial enough to be asleep by early evening. There were no lively bars here, no "after-hours" clubs. Discotheques had been declared emphatically illegal and a public nuisance by the bureaucrats of the socialist government. Loud music was detrimental to the reverent historical atmosphere, they declared, and that was that.

It was here in quiet, provincial Sintra that we intended to plant ourselves, in the deep forests and embracing climate of the Sintra mountain range. We had given in to the historical allure that so many visitors had been unable to resist. At times populated by the Romans, Moors, and British, Sintra had been the summer resort of the kings of Portugal since the thirteenth century. With them came their retinues plus sycophants and hangers-on, and it was these lesser members of the court who had built the great manor houses that lent Sintra its distinguished, almost regal air. And no less than three castles graced the rocky hillsides. It was an ennobling collage, we thought, this architectural museum set in a lush forest that tumbled from the mountains down to the sea.

Although removed from chaotic Lisbon by only a few kilometers, Sintra was total tranquillity. At day's end noisy tourists returned to Lisbon, Cascais, or Estoril, the "glitter" centers where they could exhaust themselves gambling, eating, or drinking late into the night. Sintra yawned at dusk, and its residents, with few exceptions, were sleeping soundly by 9:00 P.M. It was the perfect setting for our future lives, we had decided after lengthy discussions about other parts of the country. Nowhere else combined the requisite elements of sun, sky, atmosphere, and opportunity.

If only it would stop raining!

Had we made the right decision? I wondered. And I knew the same thoughts were running through Barbara's mind as we drove through dark, cobblestoned streets, searching for the Hotel Central, our chosen base of operation. The storm had obviously caused some difficulties here. Large tree limbs and downed power lines almost blocked our passage at several intersections.

Although it seemed to be not at all where I remembered it, we finally found the hotel. At first glance it didn't appear open, but then, with no electricity, all of Sintra seemed to be in perpetual mourning. As I left the van and approached the hotel, I noticed some sort of strange radiant light coming from within. The entrance foyer was lit by several scores of candles. And inside, everything was as quiet as a catacomb.

I cleared my throat several times, hoping to draw someone to the reception desk, an ancient oak cubicle pushed against one side of the foyer. There was the smell of mold in the air, moldy mold, judiciously aged mold, Sintra mold. I convinced myself that I liked it.

I heard a slight scream and turned around. Behind me was a young girl, a look of abject terror on her face.

"*Boa tarde,*" I said.

She made no immediate response. She simply stared at me, and I suddenly realized the cause of her alarm. I had forgotten to remove the towel I had wrapped around my head. I reached up and pulled it off. "Our roof," I said lamely, "it leaks. . . . I believe we have a reservation."

The grimace on the girl's face slowly disappeared. She cocked her head to one side, assuming the universal posture of complete incomprehension. I kicked myself mentally for having spoken English. The long hours on the road had dulled me. "*Acho que temos uma marcação?*" I said, giving her our name.

She immediately straightened up. "*Oh, desculpe, senhor. Um momento.*"

She retreated slowly to a position behind the reception desk, then took down a huge, dusty book from a shelf and consulted it warily. A large sign just above her head read ONE HERE SPEAKS ENGLISH.

After a moment she closed the book slowly and said, "*Desculpe, mas não temos nada do momento.*"

I raised my eyebrows. They had nothing? No rooms? How could that be? We had called just a few days before.

She shrugged her slender shoulders. "The holidays," she explained. It was the day before New Year's, and people had made reservations far in advance. Then there was the power outage, she added. More than twenty-six hours without electricity, and the rain continued. And of course there was no one to do repairs since everyone was on holiday.

I was insistent. Was there really nothing? Not even a warm broom closet? They must have our name noted down somewhere.

"Nothing at all, sir," came the response. "And we don't have your name. If we are full, it would be impossible to make a reservation, no?"

As I contemplated the logic of her remark, the girl came out from behind the reception desk and paused to blow out several candles that had burned precariously low. "But perhaps the Tivoli next door," she said. "It is very big."

We knew the Tivoli. It was a monstrous mass of reinforced concrete, a total affront to the senses and the wonderful vernacular that was Sintra. It was overpriced and overugly, and we had sworn never to patronize it.

"Or," the girl said, "there is a new inn, not a government-owned one but a private one. Run by an *estrangeiro,* a foreigner. It's just up the hill, and since it is so new and no one really knows about it yet, perhaps . . ."

It sounded perfect. I thanked her as I backed out the door, towel in hand, bowing for some unknown reason. In the van I gave Barbara a brief report as I started the motor and within seconds we were in front of the inn, a rambling turn-of-the-century cottage with a massive chestnut tree in the front courtyard.

Barbara peered through the window with mistrust. "This is it?" she asked.

I pointed to a freshly painted sign: QUARTOS, ROOMS, CHAMBRES, ZIMMER—AT ANY HOUR.

Barbara opened her door. "I'm concerned about what 'At any hour' means, but I'll check it out."

"Just make sure to leave your turban behind," I cautioned.

She returned a few minutes later with a guarded report. Yes, they had a room, but she hadn't seen it because there was no light.

"It has to be better than sleeping in the van," I said.

After we had checked in, the jolly Dutch manager showed us to our room with a flashlight, which he generously left behind. There was no electricity, so of course there was no heat or hot water. Taking turns with the flashlight and shivering with cold, Barbara and I put on dry pajamas and dove under the covers of the bed.

I could hear the rain still pounding on the windows as I tried to get to sleep. And all I could think about was why, of all the many warm and beautiful places on the planet, we had chosen Portugal.

A very small country, on a map it looks like no more than a blunt loaf of bread attached to the broad Spanish plateau. But even though no insurmountable barriers separate it from its neighbor, Portugal is a land apart. Isolated, it is not cut from quite the same fabric as the rest of Europe. Flanked to the west and south by the Atlantic Ocean, it may not be a large country by any standards but the uniqueness of its geography is out of proportion to its size. Portugal is a country of contrasts, of harsh mountains and fertile valleys, of undulating, sun-baked plains that lead to miles of rugged coastline thrashed by an unruly ocean.

And here lives a short, stocky race of people—"children of the light," Luíz Vaz de Camões, the national poet, called them, and when we first came to know them, we began to understand his meaning. For even though buffeted and cajoled by the vagaries of history and time, the Portuguese have nevertheless maintained a certain childlike pleasure and glee in the things that surround them. True, the glories of the Age of Discovery have waned and Lisbon is perhaps no longer "princess of the world"; nevertheless, there still lingers a certain grandeur and mysticism that has never completely eroded. But to rediscover this aura is not easy. Portugal, it seems, has always been one step beyond the confines of the grand tour—that, or else it is too politically unstable to support the delicate infrastructure of mass tourism.

Thus these once proud ocean explorers, with their brief but faded majesty, have been relegated to the back burners of history, into a neutral zone where for centuries the continuum of life has remained unchanged. Even after suffering through the arduous Antonio Salazar dictatorship of the twentieth century, the Portuguese reemerged as amiable and ebullient as ever. But this somnolent country, dormant for centuries, remains relatively unexplored and unmolested. The triumvirate of church, land, and family abides, perfectly preserving the land known as the "garden of Europe."

Barbara and I had explored a good deal of this emotional landscape a winter ago when we arrived to settle temporarily into the small part of a large mansion in Sintra. Here we had found an invigorating mountain climate along with a coterie of rather eccentric but artistically inclined friends. Our few months there in what Lord Byron called the "glorious Eden of Sintra" had passed all too quickly. We hadn't had time to tire of walking the rough, uneven cobbled streets of the village or of exploring its gardens, plush with gardenia and oleander. The mimosas had pushed forth their bright yellow blossoms too quickly for us to appreciate them properly. And the Portuguese themselves had just begun to fascinate us with their combination of outward grace and inscrutable logic.

When it came time to return to New England, we felt as if we had merely been teased. I hadn't finished my Portuguese lessons, and Barbara had just begun to paint a colorful series of Portuguese scarecrows. And the winter we had experienced was so sunny and glorious that we could only imagine the pleasures summer might bring when gardens became a riot of colors and scents (we had been told) and the ocean warmed enough to allow bathers to play among the crashing waves.

But it was our new circle of international friends who put it to us more succinctly: Why return to America at all? What on earth were we doing there that we couldn't do more gracefully here? Renovating houses? How silly. Why, there wasn't a house in Sintra that didn't need repairs, they pointed out. We were forced to agree. And Barbara's art could only thrive here among the profusion of castles, mountains, forests, and beaches. Artists had been dragging their easels to Sintra for years, our friends reminded us.

At first we had resisted such an idea. But back in New England, caught up once again in our hectic, seemingly pointless summer scurry, it suddenly became apparent to us that it was time to emigrate, time to give up what had become a frantic routine of conflicting schedules and overtime hours. Huge chunks of our lives were slipping away from us as we spent every waking summer hour trying to make enough money to sustain us through the long—and at times brutal—New England winter. More and more we came to think about Sintra—its beauty and its easygoing ways. Our lives might be calm and meaningful there. In Portugal, we had come to learn, life centered around the very nobility of living. Extraneous factors such as bills and deadlines, those very entities we based our American lives on, were somehow subliminally filtered out of the mind and forgotten.

In Portugal, we thought, we could put our talents to work and still spend time with our newfound friends. We could escape seasonal depression and the dreary New England winter landscape. We could lead a more pastoral life, even plant a garden in the frost-free Portuguese climate. But most important, we could shed our American neurosis about schedules and appointments. We could gather up the pieces of our fractured, sporadic lives into something with structure and dignity.

The more we talked about it, the more we became convinced that our better selves resided in a simpler, more rural locale. Sunny Sintra with its palaces and lethargic old-world ways was to be our destiny. To do anything less, we told ourselves, would mean that we lacked imagination.

But now on the edge of sleep, I realized we had entered a different reality: It was damp and cold and without modern conveniences. Our plan was to buy and renovate an old house here. Were we mad? We were outsiders in a land where few foreigners had dared to tread. I had often had trouble communicating my wishes to crusty Yankee carpenters and craftsmen, set in their own ways. How would I fare with Portuguese workmen who lived, I was sure, in another century? My mastery of the language was far from complete, and Barbara spoke only a few words.

And what of the Portuguese bureaucracy? It was infamous. All of our friends had warned us that it was omnipresent, intractable. It governed the lives of the people with rules and regulations so arcane that even the bureaucrats themselves didn't understand them. Barbara and I were surely courting disaster by sinking every penny we had into this foolish adventure.

Barbara moaned softly in her sleep, and I suspected she was having the same dark thoughts. We had had many other adventures together, at home and on our travels around the world. My one comforting thought was that, whatever might happen to us in this strange land, Barbara would be there to share it and provide her own unique analysis of the situation. But I finally fell asleep that night convinced we had made the biggest mistake of our lives.

Pena Palace

2 THE NEXT DAY DAWNED CLEAR
and cold. Very cold. And since power had not been restored
during the night, there was still no heat in the room. Now the
morning light filtered through the windows, revealing small
clouds of steam rising off our bedcovers. And moisture was
condensing on the windowpanes in rivulets that streamed down
the glass and pooled on the floor.

But all of this was of little consequence. My dark thoughts of the night before were forgotten. Our new life lay ahead! Throwing off the chilly blankets, leaving poor, shivering Barbara behind, I dressed and went out to the streets of Sintra. This was more like it, I thought as I emerged into the bright sunlight. This was what we had come here for. This was glorious, the Portugal we had dreamed of—ethereal blue skies and eternal sun.

Walking down the green municipal gardens, I caught sight of the majestic monuments we had become familiar with during our brief previous visit. Here, across a gentle green valley full of acacia and hibiscus, was the large, somewhat plain, alabaster facade of the Paço Real, the royal palace, begun in the fourteenth century and completed in a hodgepodge of Moorish and Gothic styles. Its two massive, conical kitchen chimneys pointed upward into the cloudless sky. The palace was the centerpiece of the village, filling the main town square, the Praça da Republica, with its bulk, towering over the collection of shops, restaurants, and hotels that surrounded it.

I could see above the town, on a hillside, the sturdy walls of the Castelo dos Mouros—the moorish castle—its stark crenelation throwing rigid shadows across the rugged granite outcrop on which it perched. Then, from another angle, the Disney-like Pena Palace appeared. It was the crown jewel of the Sintra mountains, its gilded domes and haphazard architectural sprawl gleaming under the stark winter sun. Although constructed in the nineteenth century, it was built to look old. A mock castle, it included every appurtenance necessary to evoke the medieval: drawbridges, moats, statues of Turks holding candelabra, all to satisfy the fancies of a German prince consort. Surrounding the castle was a forest park no less whimsical. Its mini-fortresses, monuments, camellias, redwoods, and cypresses enhanced the suspicion that all of Sintra might have been built by mischievous children bent on having fun during their summer holiday.

As I strolled through the town, I noticed the garden paths

were thick with eucalyptus leaves and cedar needles knocked down by the storm. There was a luscious, clean smell of fresh water and pine, tempered by the ubiquitous signature odor of Sintra—mildew. It suddenly occurred to me that perhaps, besides renovating houses here, we could open a potpourri factory. There were so many opportunities, so many unknown resources to be tapped. It would take only energy and a little initiative. Those pessimists who had warned us of the hazards of trying to do business in Portugal must be wrong. How could any bureaucracy be inscrutable and stifling when surrounded by such beauty?

At the Café das Queijadas, with its bright yellow awnings and sidewalk tables, I ordered a *bica,* a small, thick beverage that seemed to consist of several teaspoons of coffee grounds with only a tongueful of liquid. The morning *bica* was a national ritual, as was coffee drinking in general. Like the Italians, the Portuguese had concocted a seemingly endless number of coffee recipes and variations, some so similar that only a gourmet's discerning palate could possibly tell them apart.

The young waitress in a starched, white apron began to apologize and bemoan the lack of electricity when suddenly, with a loud snap and crackle, the system sparked back to life. Auspicious indeed! I only hoped that I had left the heater turned on back at the inn so that Barbara could emerge at some point from the warm prison of her blankets.

As the young girl served the coffee, I asked to use the phone. I had decided it was time to strike. The hour had come to begin our endeavor. I pulled the card of a real estate agent out of my wallet and dialed the number. It seemed to ring interminably, then was abruptly answered by a young child who began to speak in a very rudimentary Portuguese. He suddenly dropped the receiver and a strange succession of sounds followed, varying from muted barnyard noises to the high pitch of a domestic squabble. Finally came the voice of an obviously perturbed woman.

"Hello! *Está!*"

"Sara?" I asked hesitantly. "Is that you?"

There was a deep sigh at the other end of the line. "Who's this? Do I know you?"

"Yes," I replied. "It's Rick. We met last year. I'm an American. Maggie introduced us."

The answer came flatly. "I don't remember."

"Your dog," I said, "bit a hole in my Levi's."

"Ridiculous. My dogs don't bite."

"Yes, of course they don't," I said. "That's just what you told us last year. We were the ones who were thinking about looking for a cottage to renovate."

Her tone suddenly changed, became more mild. "And?"

"Well, we're here now. Returned to do it."

"Oh?"

There was a short pause. A baby wailed in the background. "And you're serious now?" Sara inquired. "This time?"

"Well, we were serious last time. But we were"—I searched for the word—"underfunded."

There was another audible sigh. "Well, things are expensive now, you know."

"That's what we wanted to find out."

The waitress at the bar was staring at me, trying to make out what I was saying. She shifted some fresh *queijadas*—little sugar-cheese pastries—onto a plate. They looked very appetizing. I tried to remember their taste while waiting for Sara's response.

"Sara, are you still there?"

"Yes. You know, I still don't remember you."

I thought for a moment. "Well, as I remember, you weren't feeling too well that day. You had just split up with your boyfriend the night before at a party. I think you told us you had too much to drink and—"

"And," Sara interrupted, "you're serious about buying? You're not going to waste my time? A lot of tourists do, you know. They think it's all part of a fun vacation, going around to look at houses for sale. Small, quaint, local color museums that don't charge admission. That's how they see it. If I could tell you the number of times I've taken people out to look at properties when they had no intention of buying—"

Sara stopped talking suddenly and yelled at someone. I took another sip of my *bica*, noting that I was getting perilously close to the muddy bottom. Outside the café, horse-drawn carriages rumbled past, heading for the center square of Sintra to await the arrival of the first tourists.

"Sara?" I whispered into the receiver.

"All right," she responded. "You want to see some properties. When?"

"Well," I said with guarded optimism, "we were thinking about today."

"Today?" she said, retreating to her perturbed voice. "That's impossible. Today's a holiday."

I did some quick mental calculations. "It is?"

"Well, almost," she said. "Tomorrow is New Year's. Nobody really works today, or this week even. In fact, very few people work all this month."

"Oh."

"I mean, I can't just drop everything and go out."

"No, no."

"You must understand."

I didn't but said that I did.

"But you're really serious, seriously serious?" she asked.

"Oh, yes," I replied. "We're very serious. But of course we would prefer to see the property before we pay for it, if you know what I mean."

There was another long pause punctuated by the sound of breaking crockery in the background.

"Well, all right." Sara was back. "I'll see what I can do. I do need the money. Manuel's just taken off again. Left me without a crumb, the bastard."

I wasn't sure how to greet that announcement. "Oh, sorry."

"Do you have a car?" Sara asked.

I said yes.

"Good, we'll have to go in your car. Mine's in the shop. And we'll have to bring the baby, of course. Is that all right? Good. Let me check my list to see what's available. You know where my place is? Come up this afternoon. But only if you're really serious."

I insisted one last time about the gravity of our intentions, then rang off. Having finished the mini-coffee, I set the empty cup on the counter, paid for the call and the coffee, and then went outside into the brilliant sun. A few tourist buses had already found their way to Sintra, discharging their camera-laden Japanese and European passengers. I noticed that a long line of Portuguese women had already formed at the pseudo-Moorish fountain, an ornate affair of chiseled stone and blue tiles. Here they rallied for position with containers of every size and shape, filling them with the highly touted, rumored-to-be-miraculous water that flowed from the stone spigot. Sintra had several of these fountains, each said to possess the ability to cure a different obscure ailment. Indeed, the health of the Portuguese nation seemed to balance on the fulcrum of water and wine.

Back up the hill at the inn, I found Barbara wandering the halls, dressed in layers of heavy clothing.

"What are you doing?" I asked.

"Looking for coffee, what else? Have you seen him? Hank, the manager. Whatever his name is. He promised us breakfast. Where did you go?"

"Into the village to set up an appointment. And no, I haven't seen him."

"It's so cold. I didn't want to get out of bed. And that stupid heater. We have to find him. I've looked in the kitchen. There's no coffee. Only some dead mice."

"He's probably gone off to get you some."

"I don't think so. I've been searching for hours."

I took a hard look at Barbara. Thermal underwear, a bright

red caftan, several scarves, knitted booties. "Well," I commented, "if he saw you dressed like that, I suspect he's in hiding."

"Very funny. But can you find me some coffee? Somewhere. Please."

"I know just the place. Get dressed and come on."

·

THE HOTEL CENTRAL'S DINING ROOM WAS BUSTLING WITH ACTIVITY,
full of families spanning several generations. There were wizened
elders, propped up in armchairs and fending off legions of loud,
impudent children. Meanwhile, the middle-aged mothers and
fathers attempted to retain some measure of decorum as they
went about devouring their continental breakfasts of hard rolls
and thick black coffee. It was a ritual enacted every morning
throughout the country. We were the token foreigners and glad
to be there.

I had spent several minutes upon our arrival haranguing
the desk clerk, who was so impressed by my insistence on
booking a room that he finally granted us the privilege. He told
us to check in the following morning, and I gave him my driver's license to facilitate the transcription of my odd but amusing
foreign name. He returned it along with a somewhat wrinkled
confirmation card that I tucked away in my pocket. The clerk
had even shown us a room just to whet our appetites, petting
the ancient steam radiator proudly and assuring us of the abundant heat available at all times.

Even more important for this morning, a huge pitcher of
coffee had been placed in front of Barbara. Her sleepy face was
fading quickly as she gazed out the window at the ineffable
beauty of the Royal Palace, its clay-colored core bright under
the brilliant azure sky. It was the perfect time to tell her that I
had arranged to look at several select cottages that afternoon.
She listened attentively but bristled suddenly at the mention of
Sara's name.

"The real estate agent?" she asked.

"Yes," I answered.

"But she was the one we were warned about. She is totally unscrupulous. She inflates prices and never comes to closings."

Perhaps so, I said, but we had several advantages over other, less wary clients: our (my) ability to speak Portuguese, coupled with the fact that I was a building contractor and renovation expert. "She won't be able to slide anything by us," I said, hoping it was true. "Besides," I added, "she's the only real estate agent in the area. We're forced to deal with her."

Barbara continued to protest, pouring herself another cup of coffee. Then, joining every other adult in the room, she lit a cigarette.

"I don't know," she said. "I think we should wait."

"Why?" I asked.

"Well, I mean, we just arrived. I think we should relax for a while first. Get some perspective."

I had heard this argument before and presented my views about the rewards of quick, decisive action—all the more important now due to the high value of the dollar, not to mention the current slump in the Portuguese housing market. Improvising freely, I even made up something about holiday torpor and post-Christmas financial fatigue.

It seemed to be having some effect, and Barbara's protests grew less forceful.

"Besides," I said, adding what I hoped would be the coup de grace, "the sooner we get started and finish, the sooner you can dedicate yourself to your easel and art."

She finally agreed and asked the waiter for one last pitcher of coffee.

The Cottage

3 THE ROAD TO PENEDO WAS
arduous, and our poor blue van lurched through numerous potholes in the narrow lane. But the vistas were magnificent, the
Atlantic Ocean spreading out below us on three sides of the
Sintra peninsula. Slapping up on the rocky beaches, it threw
huge, billowing cascades of white foam high into the air. We
were ascending green hills of pine and eucalyptus that alter-

nated with erratically terraced vineyards where, we knew, the highly touted wines of Colares were grown.

We passed through the central square of Penedo, a small village with the requisite fountain standing on a cobbled terrace. The square was crowded with men drinking coffee and smoking, their coats thrown loosely over their shoulders. They regarded us with practiced curiosity. Even the basking dogs managed to lift their heads and sniff the air suspiciously.

We finally found Sara's rocky lane and were immediately greeted by two very hostile Rhodesian Ridgebacks, baying at us from either side of the van. We stopped and, afraid to get out, honked the car horn repeatedly. After several minutes Sara appeared, just as flustered as she had been the year before. She was a very attractive woman, English, with what Barbara called "perfectly chiseled cheekbones." Her eyes were green-gray, and her skin was the color of young olives. The rumor was that Sara had been in Portugal for decades—hard to believe since she was only in her mid-thirties. Apparently she had once come on vacation and stayed, working as a liaison between foreigners in search of accommodation and Portuguese willing to part with their houses for the summer months in order to earn hard currencies. This had evolved into negotiating the actual sale of properties for those intrepid few who were foolish enough to buy.

Sara approached the van now, carrying her new baby wrapped in several tattered blankets. Yelling something at the dogs, she slid open the rear door and climbed in.

"Hello," she said. "I remember you now. How are you?"

I replied that we were fine, somewhat disconcerted still by the storm the day before but definitely ready to begin our adventure.

"You've had a baby," Barbara commented.

"Yes," Sara replied. "I must have been very near pregnant when you were here last. Oh, I don't know. It's so hard to keep track of time in this country. But I've thrown that bastard Manuel out again, and this time for good. Imagine, he told me he spent the night drunk, sleeping in his car. But I knew where he'd really been. What type of cottage did you have in mind?"

Feeling invited back into the conversation, I briefly explained our prerequisites—beautiful, cheap, ruined.

Sara nodded, her high cheekbones framing almost a smile. Her eyes seemed to twinkle. "Don't get many calls for that type of thing. A ruin anyway," she said.

"We hope not," I replied.

"But I know of a few things," she added, unbuttoning her coat and blouse as she spoke. "Just turn right out of the driveway."

Inching forward between the dogs, I glanced in the rearview mirror to see Sara extract a heavy breast and plop it into her baby's mouth.

Several hours and numerous potholes later, we decided that Sara's true goal had been to take us on an extended cross-country tour. Besides visiting several of her friends, doing her shopping, picking up her laundry, and stopping at two medieval-looking pharmacies, we were treated to a viewing of a succession of houses for sale, each more elaborate and expensive than the one before. More frustrating, they were all in a state of perfect repair. I had attempted several times to remind Sara that what we wanted to see were ruins—crumbling, old, unloved houses full of potential. I had no success. She was determined, she told us, to show us all levels of the market. And who knows, Sara continually pointed out, we might find something that suited us perfectly and needed no repairs at all.

I pulled off the road after visiting the last house, an odd affair that seemed more of an architect's afterthought than a real residence. It had six-foot ceilings in all the rooms and the ugliest bathroom tiles we had ever seen plastered all over the front facade. Sara labeled it quaint. I called it a bunker fit for the Antichrist. As we sat on the side of the road, I attempted to clarify our position one last time: We had limited resources and wanted to restore a ruined cottage which was really all we could afford.

Was Sara listening? I couldn't tell. She had immediately taken advantage of the stop to again plug a breast into her wailing infant's mouth. I began to worry that the baby might be in danger of drowning in mother's milk. Then Sara clucked her tongue and stared off into the distance. "Oh," she said. "Then you're really serious about that. I thought you were kidding. It's tedious work, you know, restoring houses here. You have to be awfully careful."

I was well up to the task, I assured her. I was, among other things, a licensed builder.

"Oh it's not that," Sara responded. "I mean, you have to hire some Portuguese. Otherwise, well, they just don't do things here the way they do in other countries. I don't know how to explain it exactly. But it isn't easy."

The baby burped, and we all stared at it for a moment. The afternoon sun had begun to lower in the sky, hovering over the ocean off in the distance below us. Then at the side of the road next to us I noticed a small white cottage, smoke just beginning to emerge from its tall, rounded chimney. The house had a little entrance portico with stone columns and windows painted a vibrant yellow. It was just the style of house we wanted and was proof that they did exist. I thought about leaping from the car and throwing myself at the owner's mercy, making him an offer he could not refuse.

Sara finally let out a deep sigh. "All right," she said. "I know of something. A little cottage in a village near Sintra. It's probably what you want. Actually, Manuel and I were thinking of buying it ourselves, but now that he's gone again . . ."

I had the van in gear before Sara had finished speaking. And as we bounced down the cobbled lane, the baby's head ricocheted off Sara's bosom like a rubber ball.

Moments later we were in the middle of a very small, rustic village perched in a neck of the Sintra mountains. We had seen a sign that announced the village's name as Eugaria, and there couldn't have been more than twenty or thirty houses, most of them whitewashed and in various states of disrepair. One was for sale, and there was no doubt about it: It was just what we were looking for. Standing by the ruined wooden gate and looking down the narrow dirt path in front of the small cottage, I couldn't help but express my jubilation. "This looks wonderful," I said, noting in particular the crumbling white walls and the rotted windows. "Lots of possibilities."

"I think it looks terrible. It's probably been abandoned for years," Barbara countered, staring at me as if I were mad. Was I? She pulled a chunk of plaster off the corner of the cottage. "And the place is falling apart."

"Well, you said you were looking for a ruin," Sara said, shifting her baby in her arms.

"There are ruins and there are ruins," Barbara said. "This is more like Armageddon. Besides, the house is right in the middle of the village, and I don't like the way everyone was staring at us."

"They weren't really staring at us, I don't think," I said, knowing full well they were. It had made me nervous, too, but I refused to allow it to let me overlook the perfection of the little uninhabited cottage.

"Look on the bright side," Sara said. "If they take this much notice of any stranger who comes here, at least you'll never be robbed."

I mentioned what a good point that was, even though I was totally unconvinced. But the crumbling little house with the rusty iron railings was irresistible. I could already see myself building a large ornamental gate with flowing double arches in place of the rotted wooden portico that now gave access to the garden. And the huge protruding boulders on which the house's walls had been built—somehow their monolithic tranquillity overwhelmed what might have passed for better judgment.

I felt a twinge of pain. Barbara was stepping down hard on my foot. "I don't know," she said, looking at me intently. "This village is a little too Arab for me. It's dirty. And it's morose. And there are too many chickens and dogs running around."

Sara obviously didn't like the tone of her remarks. "It's a perfectly authentic village," she said. "If you don't like this, you probably won't like anything I have to show you."

I knew that to be true since we had already seen everything she had to offer and liked nothing—except the little gem that stood before us now.

"Well," Sara said with a sigh. "Do you want me to try to get the key?"

"No," Barbara said.

"Yes," I said almost at the same time.

Sara rolled her eyes upward. "Let me just ask at the bakery here. Someone's bound to have the key."

Before Sara had gone three steps, Barbara protested again. "I don't like it. This village is creepy."

"But look at the view." Vineyard-laden hills lay across the valley, and the sea was visible in the distance. "It couldn't be more beautiful."

"Fine, it's beautiful," Barbara said, then dismissed it with a wave of her hand. "I just don't like being spied on."

I tried to allay her fears. "Come on, there's not really anyone watching us."

Barbara pointed over my shoulder. An old woman dressed in black was waving from a balcony attached to a house on one of the terraces above us. I waved back.

"Well, she seems friendly enough," I commented, then tried to turn Barbara's attention back to the house. "We could build you a little atelier in that room right there, and—"

Barbara interrupted. "You mean you don't feel claustrophobic here? With so many houses so close by?"

"All right, so it's not a baronial country estate. We have to start somewhere, don't we? And the price is certainly right."

"Sara hasn't even mentioned the price," Barbara responded. "She's too busy breast-feeding."

And she was right. My mental computations had been

moving quickly, too quickly perhaps. I apologized, and there was a moment of silence. "But," I began again, "wouldn't a trellis look just great over that little first-floor patio? And we could plant a grapevine at the foot of the porch there, then—"

Before I could finish, Sara came around the corner. "You're in luck," she said. "One of the owners is just down the road. He's coming right up with the key."

We had already learned to accept the succession of fortuitous circumstances that seemed to regulate the daily existence of the Portuguese, so it was no surprise to us that an "owner" had been located with such facility. We had found on our previous trip that everyone seemed to be related to everyone else in very circuitous genealogical sequences that somehow became stronger in direct proportion to the amount of money involved. Still, we were not prepared for this "owner," who suddenly drove around the corner of the dirt path astride a multicolored jumble of metal whose muffler announced it as a motorbike of some obscure design. The rider was obviously not expecting to find us blocking his way. He made a quick effort to avoid us, tipping his contraption onto its side and then dumping himself in a pile of dust. But before we could rush forward to help him, he was yanking at his helmet, a strange beige affair that resembled an eggshell with earflaps.

With his helmet off he stepped forward and offered me a hand, noticing at the last moment that his fingers were covered with a thin sheen of motor oil. He laughed, took another step forward, and embraced me in a bear hug. Backing up again he slapped me on the back, then turned to Sara.

"This is the buyer?" he whispered in Portuguese.

"*Sim,*" Sara responded. "*E o senhor fala portugues.*"

He laughed again, stretching his thin lips back to reveal a mouth almost completely devoid of teeth. He was obviously intrigued by the fact that I might speak Portuguese. He looked me up and down, then moved a step closer, mumbling something under his breath.

"What did he say?" I asked Sara.

"I think he wants you to guess his age."

He looked like an ancient gargoyle, unshaven, with bullet-blue eyes that sparkled straight through the dust on his face. I made a very polite, conservative estimate that set him cooing like a pigeon.

"*Et vous, madame,*" he said to Barbara. "*Bom dia. Comment allez?*"

Barbara was perplexed. "Why is he speaking French to me?"

"He's just trying to impress you," Sara said.

"Oh."

He took Barbara's hand and kissed it. "*Combien?*" he asked.

"I don't know," Barbara stammered. "One hundred and thirty-five."

Sara translated, and the response set him off into a paroxysm of laughter. When he stopped to regain his breath, he pinched Barbara's cheek, leaving a little smudge mark.

"Close," he said. "Very close. Ninety-one!"

"Well, he definitely shouldn't be driving," Barbara said after I had translated.

The man's animation continued. "But I'm not as old as the house," he said, walking up to the wall. "This house is very old. And very solid!" To prove his point he banged his helmet against the facade. "You see? Hear that sound? That means solid."

"*E o senhor tem a chave?*" I said, hoping that asking for the key would get us inside.

"*A chave? Olhe!*" The old man put his arm around me and pulled my head close to the lock on the gate. "Not necessary," he whispered, and gave the rusted piece of metal a whack with his hand.

He was right. The lock fell off. He attempted to push open one side of the gate with a grand gesture, but the rusty hinges snapped and the gate fell forward into the courtyard. He beamed, motioning for us to enter.

Inside the walls was a small garden run amok. The knee-high grass and the elephant-sized oleasters made it look more like something out of Maurice Sendak than *Country Living*. The old man immediately began pulling up weeds, tossing them over the stone wall. *"Um bocado de trabalho,"* he said. A little work. But wasn't it beautiful?

And it was beautiful, this little garden next to the house. There was even a large fruit tree. Sara identified it as a *nêspera,* something that had no equivalent in English, she assured us, or in any other language. Its fruit was wonderful. And it could easily be marketed for huge sums of money. But even more impressive was the layout of the little cottage. A rounded portico led to the ground floor. A wooden batten door was hanging wide open, and in the dimly lit interior we could see the dirt floor and massive stone walls that supported the structure. A rough-hewn stone staircase ascended on the outside of the house to the other floor, providing access between the two levels, and at the top of the staircase was a tiny terrace—a good place to sit and view the ocean, I thought.

The old man caught me looking at the upper floor and immediately pulled me up the staircase. *"O senhor vai gostar disso!"* He dug his fingernails into my arm for emphasis.

Whatever it was that I was going to like was behind the door he now kicked open with the toe of his boot. As my eyes adjusted to the darkness, I could make out the contours of the lovely little room inside. It had a dusty wooden floor and two shuttered windows with built-in seats. There was even a primitive band of ornamental plaster on the ceiling. Beyond this room I could see another through a crude angular doorway. I took a step inside but was prevented from moving farther by the old man.

"Com cuidado," he cautioned. "It is very old."

Sara and Barbara were at the door now, peering in over our shoulders. "What do you think?" I asked Barbara.

"I think it needs ten years of work. But it is cute."

"Maybe not that much work," I said. "Some paint, new

windows. I'd like to save that plaster molding."

I pointed to the ceiling, a ceiling that I was already beginning to regard as "our" ceiling. I tried briefly to force the waves of emotion out of my head. I had to be practical. I was a builder in a foreign land. Different rules might apply here. "How is the roof?" I asked the old man.

"Like me," he responded, beating on his chest. "Ancient but very strong."

I looked at Sara. "What do you know?"

"Oh, not much. Manuel had a look at it the last time he was around. I think he said it could be artfully patched."

"And what about electricity?" I asked the old man. *"Tem eletricidade?"*

He grinned. *"Pois tem, pois tem!"*

He carefully tiptoed to what appeared to be a fuse box, opened it up, and flipped a switch. Nothing happened. The single lightbulb hanging from the ceiling remained dark.

"Um momento!" The old man ran out the door and a moment later was back with a package he unwrapped to reveal a new lightbulb. He walked carefully to the center of the room, stood on his tiptoes, and exchanged the bulbs. Back at the fuse box he flipped the switch again. The light fluttered for a few moments, then stayed on.

The old man slapped his side. *"Tem luz, tem luz, sim senhor."*

I asked where the outlets were. He seemed confused and asked Sara for clarification. She began a dissertation that lasted for paragraphs, using words I did not know. The old man shook his head the entire time, clucking his tongue at intervals.

"He says there aren't any," Sara finally said. "That's it here. Just the one bulb."

"Just one light? For the entire house?" I asked, incredulous.

Sara gave me a half smile. "Well, it's a start. It could be worse, you know. I mean, there are still houses in this village with no electricity at all. *Não é?"* she asked the old man who was stroking his chin.

He immediately became animated. *"Sim, sim!"* he said, answering with such ferocious intensity that I knew he hadn't understood the question. I was prompted to think about another mundane but critical issue—water. I posed the question in words with the fluidity at least the equal of Camões.

The old man seemed to have expected the question. His eyes lit up, and he pressed a crooked finger to his lips. *"Com isso não ha problema,"* he whispered as if sharing a classified secret.

Since the question of electricity had been resolved in such an effortless manner, I could hardly wait to hear his clarification of the water situation. We had been warned about water problems by everyone we had encountered. Water, we were told, was seldom available, and even if available, was absent for large portions of the year. Moreover, the pressure was minimal or nonexistent. Even in areas with seemingly abundant supplies, the mains were either old or corroded or lead, or all three. It was hard to believe in an area like Sintra that abounded with fountains and springs, but we had been assured repeatedly that this was the case.

The old man took my hand now and carefully guided me around the perimeter of the room. I felt as if I was being led by a sherpa on a Himalayan trek. Under our feet, the ancient wood floor creaked and heaved noisily. As I was about to protest against moving farther, he pulled me through a doorway in the corner of the room. In the dim light of the cubicle we had entered I could make out the familiar outline of a hint of civilization—a toilet. It was shiny white porcelain and had no seat.

My mood immediately elevated, for I knew that where there was a toilet there must be plumbing—a water supply line at least, and even more important, a sewer. My mind rapidly calculated the dollars/escudos we would save by not having to install a sewage main or a new septic tank. With unabated glee I followed the old man's nudgings toward the porcelain bowl until we hovered just over it. He directed my glance down into the toilet. I stared, not knowing quite what to look for.

He smiled and patted me on the back. *"Água,"* he said. Water. He pointed to the dirty brown liquid in the base of the bowl, then proceeded to explain that although it was a total mystery to him, every time he had come here to the house he had found water in the toilet bowl—even after the toilet had been used by one of the family. He had witnessed it several times, he said. Someone would go in to relieve himself, and when he went in just after, lo and behold, the water was still there! It was a minor miracle, he knew. Clever people must have hooked the toilet up to a spring somehow. And it was good water, he said. You could see your reflection in it!

He coaxed me to examine this natural wonder, and under that pretense I leaned over to search for the tap, any tap or supply line that might lead to the toilet bowl. But of course there was none. In fact, the toilet had no tank. The previous tenants had obviously flushed the thing with a bucket of water brought from somewhere else. But still there had to be a cesspool or septic tank. I wondered what shape that was in. I also wondered what type of plumbing the old man might have at home if he found this sanitary arrangement so miraculous. I decided not to ask.

Eugaria

4 FOR THE NEXT SEVERAL DAYS the weather was majestic—short, intensely sunny days punctuated by brisk sea breezes. The air smelled of pine and salt laced with an undertone of mold and mushroom; historic, reverential air, it seemed. It was invigorating.

Our lives had settled into a basic routine. Up early at the

Hotel Central, shivering with cold, we would descend the creaky wooden staircase to the dining room. There we would order copious amounts of the seventeen different coffee variations available, experimenting blindly, sipping, dunking, conversing—all part of the wonderful ritual of acclimatization. And every morning when the owner of the Central approached to greet us, we would inquire about the condition of the heating system. Why was it that the radiators seemed to warm up only infrequently during the night, never staying on long enough to dispel the chill? Our question always met with the same response—a fatherly grin and a fond embrace followed by long exponential equations on the physics of heating. Then, of course, the heartfelt guarantee that things would be different tonight. And usually things were different—invariably colder.

But in the end it didn't matter. We had been adopted by the Central staff. Word had circulated that we intended to settle in the region, and this immediately changed our relationship with the residents of the town. What we were considering seemed to them preposterous and reckless. Buy an old ruined house here? Why would we do that? Did we know the government was fickle and unstable? That the economy was a shambles? That Portugal's glorious past could never be relived in its future? Yes, we responded, we had heard all that before—that Portugal was a tedious backwater, a third world country, intractable, wedged firmly in the gap between past and future. But, we always countered, what about the beauty, the history, the light? What about the gentle, considerate manners of the people?

Our riposte was always met with a smile and a shrug— and the firm conviction that we were totally insane.

We visited the little cottage and the village every day at a different hour. It seemed somehow important to view the setting in a variety of light. We had managed to pace the entire village now and had taken its measure. Its core was the cobbled road that neatly divided the accumulation of houses in half. From this main road issued several lesser alleys leading off in different directions, narrowing dramatically as they progressed. The houses were all whitewashed with the unique exception of one that was painted electric blue. It belonged to a famous architect, we were told. There was a Romanesque chapel and a rudimentary fountain from which elderly ladies clad in black carried blue plastic water jugs balanced carefully on their heads. We nodded as we passed them, and they invariably smiled.

Back at the cottage we often sat on the front stoop and gazed out at the ocean in the distance. We would draw renovation plans with sticks in the dirt of the footpath that ran in front of the house. The design was simple. We would clear out the bottom floor, utilized until now only for animal husbandry and wine making. Here we would locate a large, American-style eat-in kitchen with doors into the garden. Then, beyond the kitchen, we would sculpt a cozy living room out of the three-foot-thick walls, and I would build a fireplace as a source of heat. On the upper floor we had decided to enlarge the toilet cubicle into a real bathroom. It would be attached to the master bedroom, where we would set another small fireplace into the crumbling and crude hearth that must have served as a rudimentary kitchen over the last few centuries. The remainder of the upper floor would be divided into a sitting room and a second bedroom— ready to receive the multitudes of guests who had pledged to visit us when we announced our plans to move abroad.

Each day I would pretend to cast a learned and suspicious eye over the construction details of the cottage. And each day the same thing happened. I would break into a cold sweat and experience waves of total terror.

It had begun simply enough. One day while scanning the ridge of the house roof, I became convinced that it was perceptibly lower than it had been the day before. I attempted to dismiss this phenomenon as a vague fear. After all, Sara said that her absent boyfriend Manuel had checked the roof and found it in good enough shape. The next day, however, announced the sad reality. We found several roof tiles that had fallen to the ground. I knew it wasn't a good omen. Barbara looked at me quizzically. "Must have been the wind," I said in what I hoped was an optimistic tone.

Barbara scanned the facade of the house. "There's another broken window," she said. I looked to where she was pointing. She was right.

"The people in this village hate us," Barbara said. "They resent us because we're foreigners."

No, I said, trying to reassure her. That wasn't true. The window had been broken already, probably by the roving bands of children we had seen in the narrow cobblestoned alleyways of the village. The Portuguese weren't like that at all, I insisted. They're just curious.

"And destructive," Barbara added. She took a felt pen from her pocket, went to the front of the house, and drew a little red X on each of the remaining panes of glass. "We'll see," she said, putting the pen back in her pocket.

And with almost unfailing regularity, another pane of glass was found shattered daily. I would remain stoic, contemplate the scene of the crime, and then announce that the house needed new windows anyway, so what did it matter? It wasn't as if there were chicken feet and blood splattered all over the walls. These were simply the misdemeanors of youth.

Barbara stared right through me. "Right," she said. "But maybe we should buy a ruin someplace safe, like Beirut."

I, too, had contemplated backing out. Every day that we visited the village there seemed to be more disheveled dogs lying about the cobbled streets. Then one day we arrived to find the rustic batten gate we had so much admired lying in pieces where it had fallen in the garden. I inspected it. It was infested with deathwatch beetles.

"That wind was fairly strong last night," I offered by way of explanation. I looked at Barbara. It didn't seem to be working. "I have a new set of gates already planned for this opening, with a rounded portico on top and a planter." My voice went on but with no emotional conviction. In my mind I tried to determine the financial ramifications of bailing out now. Unfortunately, we had already paid a sizable deposit—in cash. Sara had quickly stashed her share in her bosom, delivering the remainder to the crusty old man who hooted three times, stuck the money into his helmet, and roared off on his battered motorbike. I had felt fairly secure at the time, having demanded that an official contract be drawn up. As the old man careened away, I unfolded the already wrinkled document and reread it. It all seemed to be in order, I noted, except the old man had forgotten to sign! I tried to yell after him but to no avail.

"How did this happen?" I asked Sara, holding up the unsigned contract.

"Don't worry. I know him. He's very honest."

"Oh, that's great, but he can't drive and he has a ton of our money under his eggshell-thin helmet."

"Look," Sara said, "there's something you should learn right away. In this country everything is difficult. So if you want to try to do something, you have to decide that you really want to do it badly."

She smiled. "Besides, the old bugger probably doesn't know how to write anyway."

At least at night, after a few glasses of the local red wine, things didn't seem so bad. Barbara and I would sit down to our steaming bowl of soup du jour, invariably some form of *caldo verde,* a rough cabbage and vegetable mélange, then sort through the rest of the vaguely medieval menu. We would watch through the windows of the dining room of the Central as the colored lights came on to illuminate the smooth stucco facade of the Royal Palace. Then, a moment later, the lights would flick on around the Pena Palace up the steep hillside, giving it an eerie glow, as if a UFO were hovering over the coast. The magic of the night always seemed to allay and soften the surreal events of the day.

As was our habit, we discussed our plans both before and then again after the consumption of local spirits. Not trusting our fate to any one wine, red or white, vineyard designated or straight from the cask, we altered the color of the wine and its region nightly to obtain a clearer perspective. After a few days of experimentation, I found that Bucelas *vinho branco,* a white wine, had the least effect on calming our nerves. We drank it at the conclusion of sunny days spent far away from the cottage. For other days when we discovered more broken windows and fallen roof tiles, there was only one remedy—aged Colares red. The wine that survived phylloxera was the perfect potion to mollify our increasingly numerous misgivings. The owner of the Central, *Senhor* João, had just opened our second bottle of Colares red one evening, and as he poured the wine, he shot me a look of commiseration that made me suppose he had figured out our system.

I took a long sip and then sighed. Things immediately looked brighter. Did it really matter that a reckless old man had a good portion of our cash riding around with him on an antiquated motorbike? That we had a contract on official government paper complete with colorful fiscal stamps that unfortunately lacked a signature? No, it didn't really matter, I told myself. So what if the man at the American consulate had laughed at us when I asked if they could help us in case of an emergency. "Buy a house here?" he said, incredulous. "We don't advise that. Unless you really want to."

But as of yet there was no emergency. We assumed that the old man would want the rest of the money—especially for a house that seemed to sink more deeply into the ground every day. Maybe. I had unpacked my construction books and looked at them again. I knew this stuff. I was sure I could handle any technical eventuality. Perhaps. Then there was our ace in the hole, the contingency clause I had insisted that Sara include in the contract—to wit that we would proceed no further until we had guarantees and an estimate from the municipal water company ensuring hookup to the cottage. We had already submitted the official request and paid the official fees—more of those lovely little fiscal stamps. It would take two weeks, we had been told. We should relax. And wait.

"*Senhor* License?"

It was the girl from the front desk. The peculiar form of address dated back to the day we had registered at the hotel. Since our last name was difficult to spell, I had made the mistake of giving the clerk my American driver's license so he could transcribe it. He had looked no further than the top line, so the official hotel registration now read Mr. and Mrs. Driver's License. Not wanting to offend anyone, I had explained that, like the Portuguese, I also went by several other names of which "Driver" and "License" were only two. I gave them my real name, but since Barbara had taken to calling me "Driver" whenever the opportunity arose, the Central staff remained perplexed.

"*Senhor* Driver?" the girl said again.

"Yes. *Sim.*"

"*Telefonema.*"

"*Obrigado.*"

I got up from the table slowly. It was late. Who could be calling at this hour? At the front desk I untangled the battered, antiquated apparatus from the plastic flowers sitting next to it.

"Hello?"

"Rick? It's Sara. I hope I'm not calling too late."

I reassured her.

"Something's come up on our deal. It seems there's another buyer. A doctor in Sintra. You and Barbara will have to make a decision very soon."

Somewhat annoyed, I told Sara that we were first in line,

that we had a contract, that we had already paid money.

"That's all well and good," she replied, "but remember I told you not to place much faith in that contract. I'm not a lawyer. And the silly thing isn't even signed. Besides, this doctor, whoever he is, has agreed to buy without any stipulations."

"What about the money?" I asked.

"Oh, you'll probably get that back. You may have to get a lawyer, of course, and then . . ."

I had stopped listening. She said something else, then hung up suddenly to attend to the baby crying in the background. I felt a sudden need for more Colares red.

Local Farmers

5 THE NEXT MORNING, PASSING
up early coffee, I set out for another visit to the water company.
After a long discourse the night before, Barbara and I had decided to attempt to force a disclosure—or at least some type of
guarantee about when we would get water. There was a saying
in Portugal that we had heard often: Disputes occur over three

things—wine, women, and water. Water was very important to us. Without it, whatever type of house we might make out of the little cottage would have no market value—something we had to consider since we were sinking all our savings into it.

Sara had advised us to drill a well, but the narrow cobblestoned paths leading to the house precluded passage of the large-scale equipment needed to do the job. Besides, the entire village was on septic tank disposal systems, tanks that were old and probably improperly constructed. With our cottage located toward the bottom of the village, contaminated groundwater would certainly find any hole we might drill. A well was not a very sanitary option.

I pondered all this as I passed in front of the Royal Palace, which steamed in the early morning sun. Taxis were already lining up to greet the early tourists, their drivers hoping to convince them that they should be conveyed up the hill to the Pena Palace by automobile. There was a strong, sweet scent of eucalyptus and smoke in the air that blended perfectly with the fragrance of the blossoming mimosa trees in the city park. As I rounded the corner of the serpentine road, the whimsical municipal palace came into view, its glossy multicolored roof tiles glistening in the morning light. In front of it passed a parade of horse-drawn buggies, freshly dressed from the stables, each a jumble of polished brass, wood, and leather rigging. Everything was so right, so ongoing, so tranquil. Historical demeanor always seemed to lend authenticity to a place, I thought as I headed in the direction of the water company. It was as if the continuing, unvarying rituals of man bestowed congruity and integrity on an otherwise random universe. Sintra was this way—unchanging and eternal. We loved it for that very reason.

As early as it was, crowds of people were already lined up in front of the double doors of the crude plaster building of the water company. They had papers clutched in their hands and jostled for position. I felt right at home since I, too, had a paper, as wrinkled and unsigned as the contract was. Nevertheless, I pulled it out of my pocket, grasped it firmly, and took my place in line.

After several minutes of waiting without seeming to move, I turned to the man next to me.

"*Bom dia.*"

He smiled like a child. "*Bom dia,*" he responded.

"Do you also have business with the water company?" I asked.

He nodded. Unhappily, yes, he said. And if I didn't have real business here, I would be better off running away as fast as possible. "Enjoy your vacation," he added.

I told him that I wasn't on vacation. My wife and I were trying to buy a house, an old house that we could restore.

He looked at me obliquely. Buy a house? Here? I was certainly crazy, he said. And an old house? Why? There were so many new modern apartments. Expensive, yes, but certainly not beyond the means of a foreigner.

I said that we were not typical foreigners. We had very little money to work with, and we appreciated the style of the older homes.

He shook his head and tapped his nose. "Foreigners always have money," he said. "An old house. Hmmmm. You are very crazy indeed." He nodded toward the crumbling yellow facade of the building in front of us. "And then," he said, "to want to deal with these people!"

I asked what people he was referring to.

"Them!" he said, gesturing toward the building. "Municipal services! *Vigaristas!* Crooks!"

"But they represent the town, don't they?" I said. "They're government."

I had a sudden queasy feeling in my stomach.

"Government, ha!" he exclaimed. "They're a bunch of communists. Thieves! At least when a robber sticks a knife in your ribs, you know you're being robbed. These people, they will kill you so softly, you won't even know you are dead!"

I stood quietly for a moment, gazing into the unmoving crowd. There was, I knew, a large collection of Portuguese political parties, each with a retinue of stalwart supporters. But long ago I had given up trying to understand their platforms. The political situation was still in chaos, and the government seemed to change every other week. But I had never heard any particular party equated directly with government agencies, so I wondered what effect communism might have on our cottage. Water was a communal resource; therefore, dividing it among the populace equally seemed fair enough. Nothing to worry about here, I thought. Still, I was curious.

"I don't understand," I said to the man next to me. "If you don't like these people or trust them, why are you here?"

He held his scrap of paper up in the air. "I have to pay the bill. Otherwise . . ." He drew a finger across his throat. "Otherwise, they cut you off. Then you have to wait years to be reconnected. Communists!"

A lady in the line turned and put a finger to her lips to caution us that "they" might be listening. The man tipped his cap to her.

"You have to come here in person to pay the bill?" I asked. "Can't you put it in the mail?"

The man rolled his eyes. "The mail," he grunted. "Trust the postal service? Rotten bunch of socialists!"

Two hours and a few odd minutes later, after having been shuffled among several *guichês*—small cluttered cubicles faced with filthy cracked glass—I found a busy bureaucrat who acknowledged that she "might" know something about our request to be connected to the water system. She was a middle-aged woman, very attractive, with inordinately long fingernails that she used like guitar picks to riffle through the mountains of paper on her desktop.

I greeted her as officially and warmly as I could, then issued my usual disclaimer about the lamentable state of my spoken Portuguese.

"Compared with Camões," she said, "we all speak Portuguese like children."

Camões was the revered Portuguese poet who had written the *Lusiads,* a great sixteenth-century epic. I had learned on my previous visit to invoke his name as often as possible because it always elicited a positive response.

I nodded humbly, agreeing, then began to explain our plight. The woman seemed to listen intently, smiling at intervals when my grammar slipped. All things considered, she didn't seem like a hard-core communist to me. Too much gold around her neck and on her fingers. I had been told that communists dressed badly and had dour faces. And they would definitely not have nails like hers. Obviously the man I had spoken to outside was mistaken.

She asked for the *talão,* the receipt I had been given when I made the original request two weeks before. I produced it, and taking note of the number, she began to sort through the files in front of her with a rapidity that would have been the envy of IBM. She found the relevant document, disappeared for several minutes, then returned and handed the receipt back to me. "It hasn't been done yet," she said.

I responded that I knew that. Then I told her of our need to clarify the water situation before we proceeded to buy the house.

"You have a contract?" she asked. "Let me see it."

I handed it to her, and she looked it over briefly, clucking her tongue. *"Mal feito."* Very poorly done, she said.

Yes, I said. It was only a preliminary agreement, an agreement to agree.

"Hmmmm," she said. "As long as you didn't give them any money."

"Oh, no," I replied, lying. "Nothing like that."

"Be careful," she said, waving a painted nail in front of my face. "It's not signed."

Pretending surprise, I looked at the blank space she had indicated. I expressed my consternation, then asked again when she thought our request might be acted upon.

"In two weeks," she said emphatically.

"But which two weeks?" I asked. Another two weeks or the two weeks that had already gone by?

She glanced at the request on her desk again. "Strange," she said. "These are usually completed on time. Perhaps you should make another request."

I tried to remain calm, but a long line of people had formed behind me and I sensed their restlessness—or at least thought I did. I decided to make one last attempt.

"So you can't tell me anything? Anything at all?"

Her mouth formed a little pout. "Oh, no, sir. It is very complicated these formulas. It takes an engineer and others to determine the cost."

I told her I wasn't really concerned about the cost right now, just with the fact that we would eventually be connected to the system.

She seemed surprised. Why didn't I say that in the first place? Of course we would be connected. Of that there could be no doubt. After all, the water company was a municipal service, owned by the people, managed by the people. Its purpose was to distribute natural resources to all equally.

Exactly, I thought. I was elated. Then there would be no problem? We could buy the house? The water company couldn't deny us?

No, it couldn't deny us, she said, unless I was a criminal or a schizophrenic.

I thanked her profusely and even tried to shake her hand but found that I couldn't fit my fingers through the small hole in the glass. I bowed instead and asked her name.

Matilda, she said. The name of our liberator.

Feeling completely unburdened now, I jostled my way through the crowd still outside the building. The house was a go again! Time to forge ahead with the plan. I would have to call Sara and tell her to notify the doctor that the house had already been sold. Adventure lay ahead—after coffee and *queijadas,* of course.

Olive Trees

6 I CONSUMED A FULL COMPLE-
ment of local pastries and congratulated myself one more time
on the morning's developments before I returned to the Central. There a surprise awaited me. "*Senhor* License." A voice summoned me over to the front desk. *Dona* Barbara, it seemed, had
left me a note. I opened it and read, "Found the perfect rental.
Join me in Varzea as soon as you can."

The road to Varzea de Colares was one of the great scenic wonders of the world. Leaving Sintra, it wound sinuously along the mountainside, passing several of the great eclectic quintas of the area. There was, to begin with, the abandoned Estalagem do Cavalheiro, its rotting windows and doors host now to a varied collection of weeds and wildflowers. It had been saved from encroaching urban development because, it was rumored, Lord Byron had lodged there during his stay in Sintra. As with all historical properties in the area, promises had been made that it would be restored to its former grandeur in the near future. Meanwhile, it crumbled artfully.

A few hundred meters farther along was the arabesque Quinta do Relogio, its Moorish arched portals brilliantly highlighted by the formal gardens that surrounded it. There were ponds and waterfalls visible from the road, all framed by tall palm trees. Also abandoned, the Relogio stood like a solemn sentinel over the Sintra valley.

Just across from the Relogio, at the corner of the road, was the most famous of the "private" quintas—the Regaleira, or, as it was called locally, the Quinta of Millions, a title that referred to its imagined cost of construction. Although of a more recent vintage than some of its neighbors, the Regaleira's complex facade had taken years to construct. It was a huge edifice, rather like a wedding cake frosted by a madman. The detail was extraordinary. There were ropes and seaweed, floral rosettes and intricate vine work all cast in stucco and applied above doors and windows. We had been told that the gardens were full of caves and bats, and that the whole complex was for sale for a million dollars cash—a bargain as real estate went, but given the political situation, perhaps still risky business.

Farther down the narrow mountain road, on a flat promontory overlooking the entire Colares Valley, was the Hotel Palácio do Seteais, its semiclassical facade a sharp white in contrast to the acres of manicured lawn in front of it. It was a grand sixteenth-century structure with monumental arches, urns, and awnings, all surrounded by citrus groves. Its pretentious physical appearance was carried over into its imprudently enforced "French" ambience. As I drove past, I recalled a birthday dinner there from the year before: the vast, empty dining room with its lovely floral-stenciled walls; the unchoreographed slapstick of the several waiters futilely attempting dignified service; the maudlin pianist pounding out renditions of a pan-European repertoire. It had been wonderfully archaic—a birthday sequence completely out of time, as perhaps all birthday celebrations should be.

After Seteais, the road entered a thick, moist, primeval forest—gnarled thickets of huge pine, eucalyptus, and oak towering over a lush, dense undergrowth. Little light entered here, and it was always a mystical experience passing through. There were one or two large quintas almost lost in the foliage. They were said to be haunted by spirits that threw rocks at intruders—a crude form of home security perhaps.

Farther along there were ancient fountains mixed with valley vistas, and then came the jewel of the Sintra range, Monserrate, its ornate domes jutting up from the semitropical exuberance that surrounded it. World famous for its gardens, a massive collection of rare plants, it had recently fallen under government jurisdiction. It sat quietly, mournfully, its doors locked and its plants vaguely maintained. Monserrate, too, had been promised a face-lift, but with the ingrained fickleness of the political situation, little had been done.

A few minutes later I was in Várzea de Colares, a pleasant tree-lined village with multiple cafés, a police station, a meandering stream, and a Salvation Army center.

I saw Barbara sitting with Michael, a friend of ours, at one of the outdoor tables. The café was busy, the tables all occupied by people chain-smoking and conversing intently.

I found a dilapidated chair and dragged it over to the table. Michael immediately stood and gave me a hug.

"Congratulations," he said.

I looked at Barbara. "Are we pregnant?" I asked.

Michael laughed. "On your new apartment, silly."

He sat down and fitted a fresh cigarette into his ebony holder, lighted it, and inhaled deeply. An American expatriate artist, only he could get away with his many affectations, I thought to myself: the beret he always wore, the bright scarves—things outmoded in the States that somehow didn't seem so outrageous here where time stood still.

Barbara took my hand. "I've found a perfect place to stay while we do the renovations."

"Oh?" I said. "I thought we were going to try to camp in the cottage while we worked."

"I know that that's what you wanted to do, but there's no water there, remember?"

I casually mentioned that I thought I had solved the water dilemma that morning and copious amounts would be flowing freely in the very near future.

"And what about electricity?" Barbara countered. "How can we watch videos if there's only one lightbulb in the whole house?"

"I went up to see the cottage," Michael said. "And I don't think it's in move-in condition exactly."

"Two more broken windows today," Barbara added.

All right, I said, giving in. I would relinquish the idea. What was this about an apartment?

"It's perfect," Barbara said. "It's just behind the café here. It's furnished, and we can walk to the cottage."

"And how did you find it?" I asked.

"Sara came by the Central this morning. She said that it just came on the rental market, and she immediately thought of us and how perfect the location was."

"And you've already seen it?"

A waiter appeared, and I requested a *galão,* a proportionate mix of coffee and hot milk.

"No, I haven't seen it," Barbara said. "But Michael knows the apartment and the owners very well. That's why he's here—to vouch for us as dependable tenants. They should be arriving any minute. I just know it will work out. Warmer than the Central, that's for certain."

The waiter brought my *galão,* and the conversation gradually switched to Michael and his art school. It was going well, he said. Many more bored embassy wives were turning up every day, hoping that painting watercolors or oils might help to dissipate the tedium of their lives. Some of them had genuine talent, Michael added, which made his job somewhat easier. The most fun, of course, was the gossip—high-level gossip on an international scale. The CIA would do well to enroll in the Sintra Garden Art Studio, Michael thought.

Our conversation was interrupted by the arrival of a tall, elegantly dressed, very un-Portuguese-looking woman who greeted us in a very clipped and cold British accent. Barbara and I rose and introduced ourselves. Michael embraced her warmly.

She was Emma, she said, owner of the apartment we were interested in. We didn't have any children, did we? No? Good. The apartment wasn't really suitable for children. It was full of antiques and belonged to her mother who would require it for the months of July and August. Did that suit us?

I explained that we were in the process of buying and renovating a cottage up in Eugaria. I estimated it would take four to six months to complete the project, so vacating by July would be no problem.

Emma gave me a strange look, tilting her head and adjusting her scarf. When she spoke again, it was in a very regal tone. "You're buying a house here? And you're going to renovate it yourselves? I just don't think that's done."

I briefly explained my building pedigree but noticed I was beginning to sound hopelessly optimistic.

"Well," Emma said, "no matter what happens, it will make a good story. Be sure to get a contract. And be careful with the trees and shrubs. When a house is sold here, the Portuguese usually uproot everything and take it away."

At the Market

7 SOIRÉES AT SANDRA'S BUNGA-
low near Cascais were the ultimate entertainment. Attended by
international icons and the Portuguese version of the rich and
famous, her evening affairs had quickly become a staple in our
social diet. I loved these endless dinners with fine cuisine consumed while conversing with exotic, deeply tanned, jewelry-
laden women. There were men, too—tall, handsome men

wearing ascots. None of them seemed to have careers or direction. What they did have was enormous social presence. Perfectly groomed and coiffed, they were able to hold forth at length in several languages. I envied them their elegance and effortless grace. For at least a night now and then I could bask in the radiance of their gilded pretensions, listen to their stories, and attempt to follow conversations in a variety of languages. It was a world of make-believe, a world free of mundane day-to-day concerns. Work, money, sickness—these things were simply never mentioned. Instead we spoke of art, literature, golf, and, of course, travel. Everyone at Sandra's had been everywhere.

As much as I enjoyed these brief derailments from reality, Barbara hated them. She felt abashed among these people. Their glibness, the ease and style with which they spoke, it was all foreign to her. She could not easily follow their conversations. Nor was she as adept at feigning knowledge of the faraway places of which they spoke. Invariably, the seating arrangement split us up, and Barbara would be seated at a table where English was rarely the chosen mode of expression. But she did like the food, and it was always inspired. Sandra seemed able to prepare effortlessly the cuisine of whatever country she had last visited. Menus ranged from classic French *assiettes* to the latest Thai innovations.

Sandra herself was an interesting neo-European mélange. Born of a French mother and Dutch father, she carried a Netherlands passport but spoke very limited Dutch. Her other eleven languages, however, were flawless. Raised in Portugal, she was a fashion designer and had cultivated the friendship of the elite throughout the Continent. In the fall and spring, she had her low-paid Portuguese seamstresses make her latest haute couture creations, which she would then take from show to show, from Paris to Madrid to Rome. The shows were hosted by her international contacts who received substantial discounts for their assistance. It was a Tupperware party done in fabric.

Orders would be taken, outfits stitched, and the final product, bearing no labels, smuggled to its destination by Sandra's vast network of acquaintances—smuggled to avoid paying taxes, of course.

We first met Sandra through mutual friends, and almost immediately she had asked us to carry a suitcase full of dresses from Portugal to England. We had considered it only a minor misdemeanor, and as Sandra had explained it, everyone did his best to escape paying Europe's elevated import duties and income tariffs. Her dinner invitations, we supposed, were our recompense for transporting her illicit goods. And we wondered if the others present at her parties were also being rewarded for their part in this elaborate, quasi-legal fashion network. It never seemed to come up in conversation, however, and we had determined never to ask.

On this particular evening we sat among ambassadors and princesses, artists and writers, and a small but vocal contingent of sun-baked women who seemed to be walking jewelry stores. The common characteristic among all these people, men and women alike, was their teeth. Never had we seen such a collection of perfectly aligned, highly polished incisors. They seemed to glow in the dark.

I was seated next to the Indian consul who, without asking any of my particulars, warmly engaged me in conversation about the problems of the Sikhs in northern India. Barbara was seated at a table across the room that seemed to be composed of German soccer players, all gesticulating wildly. Even at a distance I could see the look of abject terror etched on her face as she nodded her head at intervals, repeating, "Ja, ja."

Sandra had just returned from Delhi, hence fresh chapouti was on the table and the fragrant smell of tandoori wafted from the kitchen. Robert, whom Sandra described as her "pseudo-husband," moved his picture-perfect smile among the tables, dispensing a vintage Quinta da Bacalhoa red. He was an artist from Los Angeles, but no one had yet seen his art. He and Sandra had married on a midnight whim, it was rumored, a double wedding with Sandra's mother. Robert was there in the role of best man, but he had obligingly become a groom on a moment's notice. It was this facility, this penchant for caprice that we envied and that made us so different from Sandra's other friends.

Having dispensed with his duties, Robert came and sat down beside me. He lifted his glass in a brief ceremonial toast, then smiled his Colgate smile. "So," he began, "you're going to buy a house here. Bravo!"

I abandoned my conversation with the consul about renting houseboats in northern India and turned to speak to Robert. Yes, I admitted, we seemed to have begun the process.

"You're lucky to have found something so quickly," he said. "And something that was uninhabited."

I questioned his comment, and Robert went on to explain that since the 1974 revolution a very strict rent control law had been in effect. Rents could not be raised beyond their 1974 level, and no one could be evicted for any reason, even if the owner of the house wished to sell or to use it himself. This controlled rent was "inheritable," he said, which meant that it could be passed from generation to generation. Therefore, few houses became available on the resale market.

That was also the reason, Robert said, for the wholesale decay of older houses throughout Portugal. Landlords steadfastly refused to pay for repairs on properties for which they received only pennies for rent. Tenants were too stubborn or poor to make improvements themselves, so the situation slowly slid into decline. Obviously, the tenant in our house had died and the building had reverted to a large family in which no one member had sufficient resources to buy out the other family members' interest in the house. Therefore, they put it on the market. A common story, Robert said. He had heard it often, for he, too, was interested in buying a property.

I mentioned that we had met only the old man who had presented himself as the "owner."

"The others will be along as soon as they smell the money, I guarantee you," Robert said. "Hopefully they won't cause any problems. It just takes one of them to blow the deal. And hopefully they won't mind selling to a foreigner. No Portuguese would touch an old house, though. They think old houses denote poverty, so they buy or rent these horrible new apartments you see everywhere. You know, the ones with the bathroom tiles plastered all over the outside. They're all very poorly constructed. Owners don't want to sink serious money into them because of the rent controls. The 'move-in' rent can't be changed. And with inflation . . . well, who knows? Anyway, excuse me, I have to begin dessert. Do you like tiramisu? Sandra picked up some fresh mascarpone during her layover in Rome."

I pondered what Robert had said, but any trace of concern was quickly obliterated by the wine—a worthy substitute, I noted, for Colares red.

We drove back to our new apartment that night after the party. We had decided to rent Mummy's flat, as it would come to be called, after a brief inspection that afternoon. It was perfectly adequate—a bedroom, a large dressing room, a small kitchen, and a delightful sitting room that looked out over the Colares River and a row of giant linden trees. There were three levels to the building—Mummy's was the middle flat. Emma, who said that she and her family would come only on weekends, lived on the bottom. Above us, in the third flat, would come Emma's sister Agnes, whom Emma refused to talk about. Before I could press her for more information, Michael shot me an "I'll tell you later" glance.

Sara had shown up shortly after, and money had exchanged hands, most of it seeming to disappear into her copious bosom. A rental contract would be forthcoming, maybe, contingent upon factors left largely unclear. Paramount was the fact that we be out by July when "Mummy" would arrive to take up residence as she had for the previous seventy years. We nodded and agreed, signed off on an inventory we didn't bother to confirm, then were given a key. We checked out of the Central and moved in. Home at last. And heat we could control. I could also give up several of the aliases I had been forced to use at the Hotel Central.

Lying in the creaky bed that night, still somewhat dizzy from consumption at Sandra's party, I thought about what we had accomplished so far. All in all, not really a lot. It took so much energy just to be human, to surround oneself with the basic necessities and comforts of life. Here in Portugal, it seemed to require an even greater expenditure of time and effort to accomplish the most minimal of tasks. Would we make it through all this? Or would we end up like Sisyphus with his intractable stone?

I felt a sudden need for another glass of wine to quench the fire of doubt in my mind. But as I started to get out of bed, I stopped myself. Could it be that I would have to become an alcoholic to finish this project?

The "Lavadouro" - Public Wash

8 THE NEXT DAY BEGAN WITH A knock at the door. Head aching, I opened it to find a Sintra taxi driver we had befriended during our stay at the Central. He greeted me and said that a letter had arrived for us at the Central, and since he had a fare coming out this way, he thought he would bring it along. He handed it to me, and I thanked him profusely, offering him some change as a tip. He refused the

money and winked at me, gesturing toward the cab parked in the courtyard. *"Alemães,"* he said. Germans. He rubbed two fingers together. Money. He would get it from them, he said. I need not worry. Germany would cover it all.

He scampered back to his cab, and I opened the letter. It was from Serviços Municipais de Água e Saneamento—the water company. Not too bad, I thought. Several days late but considerate of them to reply to our request. Now we would know just how much it would cost to be linked up to the water main—something that had to be done soon since most of the construction here was masonry-based and water was an essential ingredient of mortar and concrete.

I read the letter carefully, searching for numbers, a date, a price, the cost of the installation—none of which I could find. It wasn't until I had read the letter several times that it struck me it wasn't a letter of confirmation at all. Instead, buried in the body of the form, someone had checked a little box and written: "Ligation not possible due to severe shortages in reservoir supplies."

I couldn't believe it. The water company had said no. Just as if we were criminals or schizophrenics!

"What's going on?" Barbara called from the bedroom.

"We just got a letter from the water company."

"That's nice."

"They said no."

"What!" There was the sound of rustling bedclothes, and Barbara came marching out. "What do you mean? You said that couldn't happen unless we were catatonic."

"Schizophrenic," I corrected. "But here it is." I held up the letter. "They say there's not enough water in the reservoir."

Barbara's face fell. "Oh, no. What reservoir do they mean?"

"It doesn't say."

"What are we going to do?"

I thought for a moment. "Well," I said, "I guess I'll go back to the water company and reconfirm my commitment to communism."

Several hours later, after having gone to Sintra and waited in the interminable line outside the water company, I found myself driving to a remote location where, I had been informed, the letter of denial had originated. At the water company I had spoken with Matilda, whom I had judged to be our only link with reality. She was as cordial this time as at our first encounter. I explained to her what had happened and she shook her head in disbelief.

"That's completely impossible," she said. "We cannot deny anyone unless—"

I finished her sentence with the requisite "criminal or schizophrenic" phrase and gave her the letter. She looked at it briefly, then got up from her chair. *"Um momento,"* she said and disappeared from the office. Gone for several minutes, she returned with a coterie of her coworkers who stared at me as if I were a rock star.

Matilda handed the letter back to me. It seems, she said, that our request had been refused. But, she added, since that was not possible, I shouldn't take it too seriously. I need only find the employee who had signed the letter and remind him that it was impossible to refuse service. She was sure everything would be fine.

I finally found the installation she had directed me to at the end of a long dirt road. It consisted of several shabby dust-brown buildings grouped around a debris-laden courtyard. A large steel gate with the letters SMAS painted on it closed the courtyard and the buildings off from the road. I parked, walked through the gateway, then entered one of the buildings through the only door I could find. Inside there was a group of uniformed guards huddled around a pair of gas heaters. Some of them dozed while others read tattered newspapers. As soon as I closed the door, they all jumped to their feet.

I greeted them and then saluted, which caused great consternation. They exchanged worried glances, and the largest of them, a very big fellow indeed, approached me. He looked me over intently, put his open hands out in front of him, and said, "*Isto* . . . this . . . *companhia das águas* . . . water . . . no palace."

I assured him I knew it was the water company and that, indeed, it was exactly what I was looking for.

He stared at my lips as I spoke, then turned to his colleagues. "*O tipo fala portugues!*" he said to them, and like a Greek chorus they confirmed his suspicions that I was speaking Portuguese.

He continued to stare at me, nodding his head up and down, wondering what to do next. Taking the initiative, I unfolded the letter and handed it to him. He immediately retreated to confer with the other guards. I couldn't understand their conversation, but the letter seemed to make them very animated. They argued and gesticulated before they finally seemed to come to some sort of ad hoc resolution.

The large guard returned and gave me the letter. "*Senhor* Alberto," he said.

Good, I thought. I had been given a name. I had to find Mr. Alberto. Since there was only one other door besides the one I had come in, I began to move in that direction. The big guard immediately held his hand up to stop me.

"*Bilhete de identidade, por favor.*"

I had heard of the identity cards that the Portuguese carried with them at all times. I, of course, did not have one. But I had learned early on of the Portuguese love of paper, so I pulled my wallet out of my pocket, extracted my driver's license, and handed it to the guard.

He studied it intently, gazing first at the picture on the license and then at me. Meanwhile, the other guards had crept forward and now fought for position to view the document in question. After what seemed an eternity he spoke again.

"*Senhor* Drivers . . ."

"No." I began to correct him but thought better of it.
"Yeah. Okay, *sim*."

"This is not an identity card."

I begged to differ. It was, in fact, an identity card. It just
wasn't a Portuguese identity card. And why, I asked, was identification needed to visit a municipal installation? And, by the
way, why were there so many guards here? What in the world
were they guarding? Water? And why was there a gate? Was this
really a NATO missile sight in disguise?

I stopped my harangue as soon as I saw that the guards
were backing slowly away from me. I began to apologize, but it
was too late. One of them was already on the phone, and I
heard the word *estrangeiro,* foreigner, repeated over and over.
Then the conversation ended.

The guard who had spoken on the phone approached me.
"Pode passar," he said, more to the others than to me. The guards
repeated his words among themselves, then, seemingly convinced, they relayed the message to me. I could go in.

They all sat down again and began reading their newspapers. Tucking my license back in my wallet, I walked to the interior door, opened it, and entered. Before me stretched a long
drab corridor full of cigarette smoke. The grimy walls were
punctuated with unadorned doorways, and at the end of the hall
there was a barred window, the glass so dirty that the daylight
was barely discernible. The game of Dungeons and Dragons
came to mind.

I entered the first office, where I found only a burning
cigarette in an ashtray on top of an ancient veneered desk laden
with graying papers. In the next office there was a man sitting
at his desk, staring at the wall. He held a lighted cigarette on
which a very long ash had accumulated. My entry woke him
from his reverie. He inhaled deeply and addressed me.

"Sim."

I was looking for Alberto, I said.

"Alberto, Alberto," he mumbled. "Everyone's looking for Alberto!"

He opened a desk drawer and drew out a walkie-talkie, which squawked loudly when he turned it on. "Alberto, Alberto," he shouted into the apparatus. He then rapped the transmitter a few times on the desk and repeated his call.

There seemed to be no response. An instant later, however, another man entered the room with a second walkie-talkie and began to criticize the man at the desk. Hadn't he learned to use the squelch button yet? And he should keep the volume low. He pointed to the appropriate knobs on his receiver.

The man at the desk didn't seem to be listening. He dismissed his walkie-talkie with a wave of his hand and said, "This man wants to talk to you."

Alberto scrutinized me carefully. He was dressed in a dirty yellow sweater, I saw, and had cowlicky hair and one of those beards so heavy that shaving several times a day was not out of the question.

He finally spoke. *"Eh pa, veja lá, o senhor é estrangeiro."*

Yes, I replied, I was a foreigner. And was he Alberto?

"Engineer Alberto," he corrected me.

Brandishing titles was a major pastime in Portugal. I decided that I would play the game. "Engineer Ricardo," I stated. "Special Engineer Ricardo."

I offered my hand and he took it, shaking it loosely. Then I pulled the letter out of my pocket, unfolded it, and held it out to him. I told Alberto that I had been sent here to speak to him, and then, in my very best feigned communist manner, went on to express my concern about the equal distribution of natural resources.

He glanced briefly at the letter, nodded, and sighed. "The situation in this village is difficult," he began. "There is not a lot of water available."

On the contrary, I countered. The Serra de Sintra was full

of water. There were springs everywhere, famous springs whose waters flowed year-round.

Alberto shuffled his feet. "Maybe . . . perhaps," he said. "But the village of Eugaria is not well supplied."

"The supply is sufficient, at least according to my preliminary reports," I said, prevaricating wildly. The only thing I knew for sure was that an old pipe came down from the mountain. The old man had showed it to me on one of his visits to the cottage.

Alberto sighed again and scratched his head. The man behind the desk was sorting rubber bands and placing them in small piles.

"Do you know the tank?" Alberto asked. "Have you seen it?"

I had seen a rubble masonry tank on one side of the road. It was pretty, had a gently corbeled roof, and was overgrown with ivy. We had been told it held the water supply for the public fountain in the center of the village.

"That tank," Alberto continued, "is the source of the problem, just as it says in this letter. You see, that tank holds all the water for the village. There are already too many houses connected to it. Plus the fountain. It simply can't support another house."

It took me a while to formulate a response, but once I had begun, my eloquence was overwhelming. I began by reciting facts and figures, all totally false, regarding the several major water projects that I had engineered throughout the world. I continued with arcane formulas and ratios, then concluded with an analysis of the little stone tank in Eugaria that, I was sure, would support several more houses easily. Should I, I asked, go to my car and bring in my briefcase with the formal studies?

"*Olhe, meu amigo,*" Alberto said, patting me on the back. He pulled me out of the room and led me down the dingy hall until we came to a vacant room. We went in.

"*Meu amigo, meu amigo,*" he kept repeating. I had no idea what might come next.

"This is the problem," Alberto said. He and several others had gone to the village the previous week. A routine mission, he had thought: measure the distances required to serve the house and where to "tee" off the main branch. All simple things that he did every day. But on this particular day as he and his coworkers had stood in front of the little stone tank, they were approached by several of the villagers, and once they found out what he and his men were doing there, they called the rest of the village and demanded en masse to know when *their* houses would be linked up to the water main. Only four or five of the twenty or so houses in the village had already been connected, Alberto explained. The others simply refused to pay, he said. Sure, some of them were poor, but the majority were strict communists who awaited the benevolence of the water company, thinking they would all be connected free of charge!

But on that day, Alberto continued, they had all decided that no one else should be connected to the water main until everyone was connected. He and his men had tried to go on about their work, Alberto said, but the villagers picked up rocks and began to stone them! They were lucky to get away with their lives!

Alberto shrugged and handed the letter back to me. It had been difficult, he said. The situation was unprecedented. Nowhere on the letter was there a place to indicate that service had been denied. He had been compelled to draw a little box, check it, and write in the reason himself. There was also, I noted, no box to check for ritual stoning.

Wine Production

9 "I TOLD YOU SO." BARBARA WAS pacing up and down the narrow living room of the apartment. "The village is creepy. It's a Stephen King village. I'm sure there are vampires living in attics. Ritual stoning. How do we know they won't stone me if I walk around without wearing makeup?"

I tried to reassure Barbara. I had discovered that the villagers hadn't really thrown stones. "I told you I checked it out," I said. "They were more like pebbles. It was only symbolic."

"Right. As if size matters. Bullets are small, too."

It was no use. As hard as I tried, I couldn't convince Barbara of the triviality of the situation. In fact, I was having a hard time convincing myself. Although the residents were very cordial and gracious every time we went to the village, I couldn't shake the feeling that we were like a turkey roasting in an oven: often basted, probed to check our tenderness. Maybe those same little pebbles were being used to break the windows of the cottage. Maybe it wasn't the children at all. Perhaps we truly were "undesirables."

"I just don't know," Barbara continued. "I still think we'd be better off in the south of France."

I reminded her that we had been robbed there.

"So? The only reason we haven't been robbed here is that we don't have anything to take yet."

I poured her another cup of coffee and offered her a croissant. The morning sun streamed in through the thin curtains, casting long shadows across the sitting room. The smell of wood wax permeated the apartment, a sharp, acidlike odor that we had come to love.

Barbara stopped to take a sip of her coffee, then continued pacing. "Even the postman here is hostile," she said.

Her comment surprised me, and I asked her what she meant.

"I don't know. Every morning I go out to greet him and get the mail. But as soon as he sees me, he drops it on the ground and runs the other way. I don't think I'm that ugly, even in the morning. Am I?"

"What do you say to him?"

"I don't know. 'Hello,' I think. I say what you told me to say."

Out the window I saw the postman approaching, a short, stocky man with a white helmet. He parked his moped against the fence and, true enough, looked with apprehension at our apartment.

"Well, he's coming now, so we'll see what the problem is."

"You're going to talk to him?" Barbara asked.

"No, I think I'll stand by the door and observe. Just go and do what you usually do."

"He probably has a special delivery of rocks," Barbara commented as she headed for the door. "Maybe I should take an umbrella."

I leaned against the doorjamb as Barbara opened the door. Outside, the postman stopped whistling as soon as he saw her. In fact, he stopped moving. From my position I could see Barbara wave and greet him.

"Bom dia," she said. *"Tu não tem caralho para mim?"*

I winced and went out the door, but I was too late. The postman was already around the corner and on his moped before I could get to the bottom of the steps. I called and waved, to no avail. Climbing back up the stairs, I stopped to pick up the little pile of letters he had dropped in his hasty retreat.

Barbara stood motionless at the top of the stairs. "You see," she said. "It must be my deodorant."

"Not at all," I replied. "It's your language. I told you that mail was *correio*."

"And what was I saying?"

"You were asking for his penis. In the familiar tense, no less."

"I was?"

"I wonder what he tells his wife."

"What a stupid language. Why do they use the same word for two different things?"

"They don't. It's a totally different word."

"Well, it sounds the same to me."

"Try using *carta* next time for letter."

"Are you mad? I'm never going to leave the apartment again. What if he decides to take me up on my offer?"

"It'll be your turn to run," I said, pulling on my coat.

"Where are you going?"

"First, to try to find the postman to apologize. Then I think I'll go by the village to talk to *Senhor* Pimenta, or whatever his name is—the guy Sara mentioned, the one who always has all the keys, the man in charge of the village."

Outside it was a clear, crisp day. Even though we were two kilometers from the ocean, I could still smell it, salty and wet in the distance. I walked in front of the two cafés, hoping the postman might be hiding there. Both terraces were already busy, the white metal tables packed with a well-dressed clientele, all smoking intensely. On a huge elm on one side of the street, a man was tacking up a faded movie poster, an advertisement for this evening's entertainment at the local club. There were three other men sweeping fallen leaves with crude twig brooms, assembling them into giant piles on the side of the road. I caught the musty smell of aging wine and noticed that the huge wooden doors of the local *adega,* or wine cellar, were open. Looking into the dark, I could see the outlines of the enormous oak casks lining the stone walls. We had been told that concerts were given inside the *adega* in the summer. The acoustics were excellent, they said, and you could drink wine straight from the tap during intermission.

A few steps farther along was the cable car barn where the old trolleys were housed during the winter. In the summer they were brought out, painted and refurbished, then put on the line to run tourists and villagers down to the sea. It was this same line whose traces could still be seen running all the way up the hill to Sintra. It had been functioning up until the time of the revolution when it was sabotaged. Later, its copper wires had been pillaged by local artists to make jewelry. Little remained of the Sintra spur except the rusting iron tracks overgrown with weeds. Plans were under way to restore it, we had been told, so that once again passengers could ride from the palaces of Sintra down to the sea.

I gave up on finding the postman and began the walk up to Eugaria. Once outside Colares, the road narrowed appreciably as it cut into the mountainside. In the valley opposite were vineyards and orchards, their barren stocks etched against the vivid green grass that grew around them. The hillsides were thickly forested with pine, acacia, cedar, eucalyptus, and oak— all growing together in a gnarled tangle punctuated by giant stones. As I rounded a corner in the road, I could see the famous boulders that loomed above Eugaria. The villagers had built a cross in concrete that anchored the boulders to the hillside, preventing them, it was hoped, from cascading down on their houses and destroying them.

Eugaria from a distance appeared to be backing away from the road in steep terraces up the hillside. The whitewashed houses gleamed like pearly teeth shining in the mouth of the forest. The divergence of design of the red-tiled roofs gave the angular contours of the village a strange geometry. Each cottage had a garden, which, even though it was winter, still contained a profusion of blossoming flowers. All appeared well tended from the valley below.

It was only upon closer inspection that the flaws of the village became visible—the crumbling walls, the peeling paint. It was definitely a humble accumulation, and the cottage we proposed to renovate only a humble house. But then, we were humble people. We had neither the inclination nor the means to live as richer foreigners lived here—in large gaudy villas replete with domestic staffs. We had met some of these expatriates on our previous visit. Their conversations seemed limited to discussions of pay rates for maids and butlers. Indeed, it seemed that Portugal was a major refuge for international scoundrels who demanded the most from their domestic staffs while, in turn, paying the least.

At the bottom of the cobblestoned road that led up through the center of the village, the first house on the right was *Senhor* Pimenta's, or rather his "store." I had been directed there by a man with a donkey. The house itself sat behind a high wall overgrown with ivy, and it had ornate arched windows with matching green shutters. In the courtyard stood a large nêspera tree already beginning to bud. I entered through a sturdy concrete portico supporting an overgrown grapevine. The door to the house/store was open, blocked only by long strips of white plastic that hung down to discourage flies. Parting the plastic strips, I went in.

It was dark and damp inside, but I could make out large sacks of grain or something similar lining the walls. Above these were innumerable shelves stocked with all manner of brightly labeled canned goods. There was a makeshift wooden counter with a display case underneath, empty except for a small wedge of molding cheese. On the counter was a huge ceramic urn and an antique scale. A little box next to the scale contained polished brass counterweights. There was no cash register and no computer. A single unlit bulb hung from the ceiling. There seemed to be no one around.

I felt a sudden jab in my ribs and turned to find an old woman perched on one of the sacks of grain. I hadn't noticed her before because her vintage clothing blended so well with the burlap. She held a crooked cane in her hand.

"*Ora bom dia,*" she said.

I returned the greeting.

"Did I scare you?" she asked.

She had, I replied.

"Good!" she cackled. "That's my job, to scare people. I'm an ugly old woman, a witch. But I have fun!"

Now that my eyes had adjusted to the dark, I could see her better. And she was right. She was indeed very old and ugly. Even with a scarf wrapped around her head, I could see the deep creases and folds in her face. Her skin was weathered and leathery, and her eyes were so small they were almost lost in the topographical confusion.

"Come on, get closer to see if you want." She poked at me with her cane. "I like being close to men!"

I wasn't quite sure how to react, so I pretended to examine some of the cans on the shelves. They were all coated with dust.

"Careful," she shouted. "Some of those cans are older than I am." She laughed at her own joke and then said, "I know who you are. You're the foreigner buying the house. You better hope I like you because I'm your next-door neighbor!"

"Oh," I murmured. "Then we should introduce ourselves."

"Ha, ha! I already know your name. I'm an ugly old hag, and when I'm not scaring people, I'm gossiping. That's my other job."

I was beginning to enjoy her sense of playfulness and decided to test her.

"All right," I said. "What's my name?"

"Ricardo!" she replied.

"Very good," I said with surprise. "What's your name?"

"I'm not going to tell you! You're a foreigner and couldn't pronounce it anyway. You'd make it sound worse than I look."

I laughed. "Then should I call you 'old hag'?"

"Why not? Everybody else does."

She obviously thought this immensely funny, breaking into laughter and tapping her cane on the floor. Then she said, "Unless . . . unless you're going to be a good neighbor and throw me scraps of food and some money now and then. In that case you can call me China."

"China," I said. "Like the country?"

"How would I know? I've never been anywhere. Only place I go is to the cemetery with my husbands. I've buried a whole stack of them. Poisoned them all. You believe that?"

I said no, I didn't.

"Then maybe there's hope for you yet. When are you moving in?"

I told her that we wanted to renovate the house first and that it wasn't in very good shape.

"Huh," she said. "Not in good shape. You should see my place. But don't worry. You want to renovate. I'll draw you some plans, show you how I want it."

I thanked her for her consideration and asked her when the plans would be ready.

"Soon as I get a face-lift, that's when!"

I laughed, then noticed something moving behind me. An elderly man emerged from an inner doorway, walking slowly, hunched over, using one hand on the counter to support himself.

"Oh, *Senhor* Pimenta," China said. "Here's that foreigner who wants to live with us. I already told him there was no discotheque here!"

Senhor Pimenta drew himself up to the counter and offered me his hand. He had regal white hair, slicked back, and large, kind, olive eyes. He wore an old gray sweater buttoned halfway up.

We shook hands and exchanged greetings. "You've already met *Dona* China, I suppose?"

China replied for me. "He has and he didn't run away."

"If you buy the house," Pimenta said to me, "she will be your neighbor."

"I warned him," China snapped. "Told him it would be cheaper to buy me. I don't need as much work as that house does."

Pimenta winked at me. "She's a character. But don't take her too seriously. Now, what can I do for you?"

I told *Senhor* Pimenta that we loved the house and the village, and that we wanted to contribute to the cultural heritage by restoring the house as faithfully as possible. We intended to use it as a full-time residence, not as a weekend getaway, and we wanted to be good neighbors and friends. However, I continued, we were somewhat concerned about what had happened to the water-company employees. We were worried that perhaps the villagers, for some reason, did not want us there.

Senhor Pimenta clucked his tongue loudly and waved a finger in the air. No, no, he said, that wasn't the case at all. The villagers were very friendly people, sometimes too curious but, all in all, very friendly. They didn't mind who lived in the village. In fact, he said, there were already a few foreigners in residence. What we must understand was the history of the village. It had sprung up several hundred years ago as a settlement of domestic workers employed at the various palaces in the Sintra area. And even though many years had gone by, the village retained its modest, humble character. The people here were workers, descendants of those who had gone before them. No one in the village had a title, and there were no family crests.

He paused for a moment and took a few deep breaths. Would I prefer the light on, he asked.

I responded that, no, the semidarkness was fine.

"Light's expensive," Pimenta said. "And it harms the produce. So . . ."

Then he began again and told me that everyone in the village lived more or less at the same social level, which created equilibrium and stability. This way there was no need for jealousy, and that explained the water situation, he said. Very few houses had water service or indeed any type of interior plumbing at all. But that made everyone equal. Everyone had to go to the fountain to haul water, and the fountain therefore served to maintain an unspoken sense of unity. It was good, this sense of unity, he thought, and to preserve it, the villagers had decided that no one else should be hooked up to the water main until a project was done to hook everyone up at the same time. "Isn't that right, *Dona* China?"

"Doesn't matter to me," she said. "I only take a bath once a year anyway."

Pimenta picked up one of the brass weights and held it in his hand. So when the men from the water company had arrived, he said, the villagers had made a stand. It had to be done. The water company had been promising for years to hook up the entire village; in fact, Eugaria was one of the few villages in the Sintra area left without water and sewage services. Too small for official notice. Unless they protested. Then maybe something would be done.

Pimenta put his hands down flat on the counter. So, he said, there was really no reason for our concern. It was nothing personal at all. We were very welcome to join the village and live among the people, very welcome. The village needed more young people anyway. And as far as water was concerned, well, it would come someday to all. But he understood that we might have necessities different from the others here since we had come from a more modern country. This being the case, we could certainly dig a well if that suited us.

"A well? Ha!" China interrupted. "If you're going to dig anything, dig me a nice little grave. That's where I'll be before the water company ever gets here."

Eugaria

10

ON A BRILLIANT JANUARY day, Barbara and I began the project. We had tried to decide the matter by secret ballot but found that neither of us had the courage to vote. We did agree, however, that to hesitate would mean to lose. The money had been invested and the contract had been written—although not signed. But it no longer made sense to sit idly and draw plans in the dirt.

Water remained a concern, but another trip to the water company allayed our fears somewhat. On the most recent excursion, I had met the chief engineer, a woman named Concepção—Conception, in English—a name we found both optimistic and encouraging. She was very cordial and explained to me, while filing her nails and chain-smoking, that the water company was very aware of the situation in Eugaria. Furthermore, she declared, she had just initiated a project to put a large prefabricated tank on the hill above the village. This tank would provide sufficient capacity so that the entire village could be linked to the water system. The project would begin within thirty days.

We were elated and marked the date on the calendar in red. A major obstacle had been overcome, we felt, and we could now channel our energies in a different direction.

But what really convinced us and sealed our intentions about the Sintra area was a walk we took one sunny afternoon. We followed the cobblestoned road through the village up into the pine-clad hills. There, not too far from our village, lining the mountain's crest, were several ancient manor houses. One or two of them were deserted, their elaborate entry gates crumbling, and trees growing up through breeches in their massive walls. The other houses, however, had been more carefully tended. Set behind ornate cast-iron gates, their elaborately decorated facades announced the delicacy and craftsmanship of another, more refined era. There was something almost mystical in the way they looked—the distorted, ancient oak trees in their courtyards, the ocher bell towers with their symmetrical stucco patterns. All this set above sweeping terraces of vivid yellow grass that, in jagged graduations, rolled softly down to the sea. And there were inspired fragrances too: lemon, mock orange, mimosa, all tinged with the odors of laurel and sage and heightened with a delicate overlay of the essence of decay.

It was a formidable array of history, this panorama of

times gone by. To think that already centuries had passed in our little adopted village. And yet the same families lived on there, persevering in their ways. Up over the mountain, we knew, were even older, now uninhabited settlements with huge mono-liths and dolmens, dedicated to the worship of the moon. We were about to become a small part of this eternal progression, we thought, about to make a minor imprint as temporal stew-ards of a cottage that had already weathered several hundred years. That thought, combined with the spirit of place and the primeval aura of the Sintra mountains, made the prospect sen-sually overwhelming.

Standing on top of this ridge between mountain and sea, we could look down and view the cottage. It stood somewhat apart from the other houses and looked forlorn and sad, a di-sheveled outcast. Yet it was an essential part of the geometry of both the mountain and the village. Its absence or replacement would be an outrage to the continuity of the place. It was obvi-ous: The house needed guidance to see it through this difficult period of its evolution. We decided that we would attempt to perform that role.

And so we began that January morning. Arriving early, we set aside the rotten gate that gave access to the little garden. Then as methodically as possible we went through the house and opened wide every door and window. It would help to dis-pel the dust we were about to create, but it was also a signal of our intentions.

With the rake and broom we had acquired at a local hard-ware store, we set about organizing the ancient garbage that lit-tered the earthen ground floor. But no sooner had we begun than we heard voices outside the door. Two women were stand-ing in the middle of the dirt path in front of the house. When they saw that they had gained our attention, they greeted us.

"*Bom dia. Bem-vindo!*"

It was the first time anyone in the village had formally

welcomed us, and that left us somewhat confused. We were certainly in no position to offer tea or cocktails, but we did put down our implements and go outside. A vigorous shaking of hands took place, and the women introduced themselves. They were mother and daughter, Maria Luisa and Fátima, part of the family that owned the house.

We were very glad to meet them, we said, and asked if they knew the old gentleman who had originally shown us the house. Yes, of course, they replied. He was a great-great uncle or something like that. No one in the family could be sure anymore. He was so old and had been around so long.

Maria Luisa was dressed in the standard Portuguese black skirt and sweater. She was a small handsome woman in her mid-fifties, her hair drawn back in a bun. Her daughter Fátima was stunning, a true beauty with a mane of black hair that trailed down to her waist. We asked them where they lived, and they responded with a brief description of their house. It was one of the houses on the cobblestoned street, the one, they said, with all the scars from trucks hitting it because the street was so narrow.

"It's a very old village, very primitive," Maria Luisa said. "Your house is over four hundred years old. It was one of the first houses in the village. Just down there is the fountain, the old fountain."

I looked but could see nothing but a tangle of ivy.

"No one uses it anymore. It's too far to walk and carry water! But it's there."

There was a moment of silence, then Maria Luisa spoke again. "Well, let's get to it." We watched in shock as she and Fátima walked into the house, picked up the rake and broom, and began cleaning. Not knowing what to do, I told them that this wasn't necessary. But they just smiled and said, *"Pois, pois,"* which I had no idea how to translate given the situation.

Barbara was less concerned. "Maybe the rest of the village will show up. That would be great. We'd be done in an hour."

I gave her a perturbed look. "We can't just let them clean all this up," I said. "And we certainly can't afford to pay them. Do you think they want to be paid? Why are they doing this?"

"I don't know. But let's go have a coffee and come back in a few hours and see how they're getting along."

We joined them in the labor. There was a lot to be removed from the ground floor. Never inhabited, as was usual with older cottages, it was a place to keep animals, make wine, and store food. Here on the hard-packed dirt floor were any number of crude implements left by the former inhabitants. We moved several old barrels, pitchforks, bricks, chains, and ropes. There was a rotten wine press, several beams, and two old steamer trunks, one of which still had its cowhide veneer more or less intact. Inside was a bundle of rotten clothing. There seemed to be hundreds of bottles of all sizes and shapes, testimony to the wine press's efficiency. Unfortunately, the bottles were all empty. Maria Luisa picked up each one, brushed off the dust, then clucked her tongue in disappointment that there was nothing in the bottle.

There were also several items whose use we could not fathom. We found six rectangular stones with round notches chiseled into them, and Maria Luisa explained that they had been used as the bases for planks that supported wine casks. "Very old," she said. Then there was a series of very sharp, rusted hooks nailed into the peeled logs that formed the ceiling. These, she told us, were used for hanging animal carcasses while they were butchered. As far back as she could remember they had raised pigs here on the ground floor. Big, fat, noisy ones with nasty dispositions. They had escaped several times, she remembered, which always resulted in frantic chases around the village. Once they were all rounded up again, they were disciplined, one by one, with a brief but intense spanking. I didn't understand the word for "spanking," I told her, so she acted it out—complete with the responsive squealing of the pigs.

But they were all gone now, she said. There hadn't been pigs here in a long time. And that was very fortunate because it took years for the smell to go away. Nasty animals, she added, but very good eating.

We had several other visitors on that first day. I had made it a point when I went to the hardware store to let it be known that we were about to start renovating the house and would need a *pedreiro*—a mason. We had discussed this with Sara and decided that it was essential to hire at least one other person to assist us, otherwise we would waste enormous amounts of time trying to locate materials and learning how to use them. The subtle word let drop at the local store caused an immediate response. By noon four applicants had already appeared. We dismissed the first three immediately. Although they professed that they knew everything about the trade, none of them was over fifteen. The other man who arrived came drunk and had to lean against the wall for support while we conducted a very brief interview.

In the afternoon came João, who insisted on pulling us away from the house to extol his virtues. He was in his thirties, dark, and not very well dressed. He told us that he would take over the entire project. He had all the tools necessary and knew all the tricks of the trade. He lived in the village, he said, and had already thought about just how the house should look when finished—a window here, a door there. It would be simple if we let him do it. And, he said, he worked very cheaply, much cheaper than the others. He could start tomorrow, in fact, and to seal our deal, we need only give him a little advance today, and he would be there first thing in the morning.

We told him that we really didn't have any money with us today but that we would consider his kind offer and give him a response in the morning. He finally said that was all right. He would come prepared to go to work early, and he was very happy to have us in the village.

As we walked back into the house somewhat cheered that we had found an eligible candidate, Maria Luisa offered us her opinion. "Be careful of that one," she said. "He's a thief and a rascal. He knows nothing about the trade and will certainly steal you blind."

"João?" I asked, perplexed. "The man we just spoke to?"

"That's him. João Ladrão, they call him. Be careful!"

João Ladrão, I thought. Jack the Thief. The title wasn't inspiring. I told Maria Luisa that we would watch out for him.

A few hours later we had succeeded in removing most of the debris from the ground floor into the little garden. There it sat, organized more or less into little mounds. Barbara and I had decided that we had to offer Maria Luisa and Fátima some money. Otherwise, we thought, we risked alienating our new neighbors.

They immediately declined, backing away from my outstretched hand, saying that they didn't want money at all. I then thought that it was only appropriate to offer them some of the objects we had removed from the house. Technically, these things really didn't belong to us. We hadn't yet paid the full amount or had any type of official closing. Several bureaucratic hurdles still lay ahead before we reached that point. These items were therefore in limbo, and we already suspected that the women were there solely to see to their disposition.

I walked over to the piles lying among the weeds and decided to offer them the objects we prized most first. Would they want, by chance, these nice oak barrels?

Oh, no, thank you, they said. Too big a thing for their small house.

How about these chiseled stone pedestals, I asked, hoping they would decline again.

Too heavy. Much too heavy. And what would they do with them anyway? No, they said, they really didn't want anything. Only to help.

Well, I said, if there was anything they wanted or if they changed their minds, they should feel free to tell us.

We both thanked them profusely, shaking hands, and they began walking toward the gate. But at the edge of the garden, Maria Luisa turned and came back.

Actually, she said, if we really didn't want them, they would take a few of the bottles.

Of course, we replied. Take as many as you wish. We had no idea what to do with them anyway. Please, feel free.

They thanked us and waved good-bye, disappearing out through the gate.

"Well," Barbara said, "that certainly was amazing. You think they'll be back tomorrow?"

"I have no idea. But we did get a lot accomplished."

We walked back into the cottage to survey what we had done. Removing all the debris had revealed some of the strange contours of the walls. There were protrusions of bedrock here and there, and some unusual forms constructed from stone and mortar. The forest of support pillars now looked more bizarre than ever. They would have to be removed soon because under them were some giant flagstones we wanted to resurrect to create a rustic floor.

We moved around the two rooms on the ground floor and discussed our plans for them. The kitchen was going to be quite large, we noted, but we would have to put some new windows in the north wall to let in more light. A little angled corner niche would make an excellent wine storage area. And there was a thick old chestnut beam lying on the ground that I thought we could use to frame an enclosure for the stove. In the other ground-floor room I showed Barbara where I thought the fireplace should go. She suggested we construct an arch to divide the living room into two distinct areas—an entryway with the fireplace and a more cozy, defined conversation area. Then, just as Barbara was tracing out the spot she had chosen to locate an arch, we heard noises coming from the garden. We made our way out through the doorway and found several people with burlap bags roaming around the little garden, stooping at intervals to pick up empty bottles and place them carefully in their sacks. Among them was Maria Luisa who waved.

"Thank you again for the bottles," she said.

The others joined in chorus. Yes, thank you, they said. And welcome to the village.

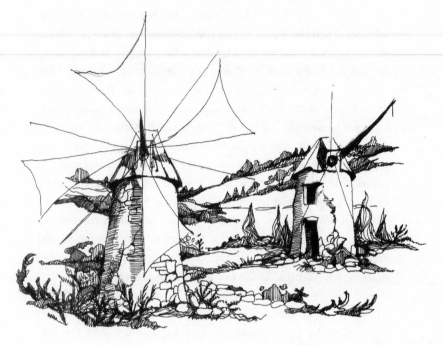

"*Moinhos*" - *Windmills*

11

A FEW DAYS LATER, AFTER A brief period of rain, we were ready for serious construction. I had consecrated a pair of Levi's to the project—ordained them and doomed them to a brief life of rips and tears, stains and burns. Barbara, too, had put her wardrobe in order, but in a different way. Organized in layers, what she wore depended entirely upon the outdoor temperature.

In addition to preparing ourselves sartorially, I had taken further steps. In Sintra I had found a hardware store that actually stocked tools made within the last hundred years. With restrained glee I combed through the aisles, sorting and selecting carefully, filling a cardboard box to the brim with the necessities of construction. I collected a power saw, levels, squares, drills, and numerous marking instruments—everything I could possibly need, I thought, to bring Portuguese construction methods into the current century. In my dreams I saw this project as a joint Portuguese-American effort. We would teach and learn in perfect harmony with those who worked with us. The exchange of knowledge would be complete and the brotherhood of man enriched. We would receive international accolades for our redeeming sociological work. Our construction designs would create a new vernacular of style. There might even be a Nobel Prize floating around in the not too distant future.

I put my fantasies on hold as I rummaged through the shelves trying to find a blade to fit the saw I had selected. When I questioned a lethargic clerk, he informed me that the saw came with a blade attached. I said that the blade that came with the saw was for plywood, and plywood did not yet exist in Portugal. He shrugged and told me that more blades would be coming in next week.

Undeterred, I packed my purchases into the van and drove back to the village. I could hardly wait to unpack and organize the little array of tools. I had never had new tools before, and possessing an entire boxful gave me immense pleasure. Everything was falling into place.

At the cottage, Barbara sat on an old trunk on the terrace, sipping a cup of coffee. I set my box down in a corner of the yard.

"Where did you get the coffee?" I asked.

"I have great news," she replied. "I discovered a café here in the village. Just down below the chapel. They let me open an account."

I was surprised. "A café? With tables and chairs?"

"And a television and a lot of flies."

I mumbled a response. "Any sign of António?"

Barbara checked her watch. "He's an hour late now."

António was the *pedreiro* we had finally hired. We had gone to João Ladrão the day after we cleaned the cottage and informed him that we had contracted another mason. We reasoned that it didn't make sense to hire someone the village proclaimed a thief. João had taken it well, almost as if he expected rejection. He shook my hand and said calmly that since he liked us so much, he had quit his regular job to work with us. And since he estimated that it would take him several months to find other employment, he thought it only fair that we compensate him for time lost. Ten thousand dollars would be fine, he said.

I wasn't sure how to respond, so I merely laughed and slapped him on the back. He then told me that I need give him only half now and the rest next week. Once I saw that he was serious, I became speechless and, pretending incomprehension, walked away quickly.

António had come the following day, the last in a long line of pretenders to the mason's throne. There was massive unemployment in Portugal, so applicants for any job were numerous. And as we quickly learned, job seekers modified their résumés to fit whatever employment was available.

I had devised a brief test to assess the basic building knowledge of the applicants. It revolved around ascertaining if a square was actually square. The first "mason" to arrive that day ran away when I presented him with the problem. The rest bungled along, giving increasingly oblique answers until I realized there was obviously some sort of networking going on. Somehow those arriving later had been informed of what they would be asked.

It was among general confusion that António arrived. He quickly dispatched Mathias, the young man I was interviewing, with a laugh and a flurry of colloquialisms I couldn't follow. Hanging his head, Mathias walked away without a word, leaving António standing alone in front of the garden wall.

Barbara and I looked him over. Even though our experience here had been brief, we were sure he was among the largest Portuguese we had ever seen. But it wasn't just his height alone. It was his bulk. He was massive. His large, pumpkinlike head sat squat on his broad shoulders. His chest and torso were as round as a whiskey barrel, and he had a large protruding stomach that would look fat on someone who didn't have his girth.

He stood with his arms crossed and looked us over, too. *"Então?"* he said.

I took this to be his standard form of greeting and approached him. Barbara whispered caution from behind me. I reached out my hand and he shook it—crushed it, rather. I was sure I heard bones break.

He introduced himself. He was António Domingos—Tony Sunday. I began to introduce myself, but António raised a hand. There was no need. He knew who we were. His grandmother lived just above us, he said. Small village, people watch. He shrugged, and the ground seemed to shake.

So, he said, when did we want him to go to work?

I was so astonished by the question that I couldn't answer.

Weren't we looking for a *pedreiro?* he asked. A real *pedreiro?* The others we had been talking to were riffraff, children, and *serventes*—laborers. If we wanted a real *pedreiro,* well, here he was.

I responded that it was a pleasure to meet him. Would he like to see the house?

No, António said. He knew the house well. He had grown up here.

I searched for other questions and amenities. Did he have any references?

He looked puzzled. I repeated the question, hoping that

the latinization of references to *referências* would convey my meaning. António said that he had tools. I tried again, explaining my meaning more carefully. António laughed and said no, he had no references. He did have friends, though. Did that count?

I asked where he had worked before, and he told me that he had worked everywhere. Well, I continued, were the people he had worked for happy?

He frowned and said that he had never asked them. But he thought they were happy, especially when the sun shone in winter and the fishing was good.

I was determined. No, I corrected, I meant were the people happy with his work?

He thought for a moment, then replied that they had never complained.

I translated for Barbara. "Small wonder," she said. "Who would dare to fire him?"

António had become impatient. Yes or no, he asked. He was busy and needed an answer.

I asked him how much he wanted. He shrugged and replied that he would work for the usual rate.

I pressed him, but with little success. The "usual" rate seemed to depend on several factors. And then there was inflation. António had become very vague.

Yes or no, he was demanding again.

I asked Barbara her opinion. "Well, at least he's incredibly strong. Maybe he can just lift the house up while we fix the foundation."

That seemed to decide the matter. I told António yes. Good, he said, and shook my hand. He offered me a cigarette, which I declined.

He repeated his offer: "*Toma.*" Take one.

I assumed that this was some essential ritual to acknowledge our agreement, so I took a cigarette and António lit it. He inhaled once deeply on his own cigarette, then threw it on the ground and crushed it with his foot. I did the same.

"*Então*," he said. "So." He would see us in three days. He had to plant some potatoes before he could begin work. Potatoes could not wait.

Yes, I agreed. Potatoes could be impatient.

He laughed. "*Ciao*," he said. "And don't worry. No one else will come to bother you about the job."

We watched him disappear around the corner of the garden, dispersing the pack of mongrel dogs that gathered there with a shrill shout. I looked at Barbara. "Don't worry," she said. "I've always trusted people who have no necks."

So now we waited for António, wondering if he would come, pondering the progress of his potatoes. I was beginning to sort through my collection of shiny new tools when I heard a knock at the gateway. It was António. He came into the garden, and suddenly the space looked very small. He was wearing the same striped shirt and dirty Levi's as the day we had met him.

"*Bom dia*," he said, taking my hand and crushing it again. "*Bom dia,* madame."

"Barbara. *Meu nome* Barbara," she said. "No 'madame.' "

"*Está bem,*" he responded. Okay. He repeated Barbara's name several times, then said to me, "So, are we working today?"

"Oh, yes," I replied.

António shook his head. "I don't think so." He looked around. "Where is the sand? Where is the cement? And how about building blocks?" He was a *pedreiro* and certainly couldn't work without the basic materials. He would come back tomorrow and check to see if the materials had arrived. If they were here, he would work. Otherwise, well, we would see.

He gave me another cigarette, lit it, and puffing on his, he walked out the gate.

Gypsy Vendors

12 LISBON WAS A SYMPHONY.
Its perfect location had attracted the Phoenicians more than
three thousand years ago. They had called it Alis-Ubbo—the delightful shore—and its natural harbor had always been lucra-
tive. Built in terraces on seven hills overlooking the confluence
of the Tagus River and the Atlantic Ocean, it was what every
large city should be—a compendium of the new and a reposi-

tory of the old. But like all capitals, Lisbon was not immune to disaster. In the fifteenth century the city was the seat of a vast, majestic empire; in 1755 it was shaken into obscurity by a tremendous earthquake that reduced it to a pile of smoking rubble. It was rebuilt, of course, but the essence of tragedy lingered. Still served water by ancient, arched aqueducts and served tourists through an expanding modern airport, Lisbon successfully straddled the centuries. It had moved forward slowly, constantly looking over its shoulder, with an aura of tainted reverence. Not grand and gaudy like other European capitals, Lisbon was more practical. What worked stayed in place, what didn't work was abandoned to the future.

Situated as the western bastion of the European continent, with Africa slumbering to the south, Lisbon had been the last landfall before sailing off into the wide blue sea. Portuguese sailors had braved the journey; its explorers had colonized the New World and returned to Lisbon with its riches. But a spirit once so grandiose had been broken, and the Portuguese had become vacuum-packed in their own traditions. It was this palpable fear of the new that had opened the gates to a lengthy dictatorship. And it was the dictatorship, harsh and conservative, that had preserved the essence of decades past, instilled formaldehyde in the blood of the people, and turned Lisbon into a bell jar of the senses.

For Barbara and me the city was a jumble of sensations. The cafés, the museums, the galleries—all were a civilized balm to the increasing rusticity of our day-to-day existence. We loved to walk in Lisbon's several public gardens, feeding the pigeons or eating a pastry under the palm and fig trees. Or else we might stroll the narrow, cobbled streets of the Baixa where the lanes were named after the trades once practiced in the stores that still lined the pavement.

If we felt more energetic, we would climb the steep hills and marvel at the eclectic vistas of rooftops, courtyards, castles, and the muddy, golden-hued river below. The noise, the traffic, and the smoke-belching buses reminded us that the New World was encroaching too quickly on the old. Here a gracious style of living—the quaint cable cars, the single-seat barbershops, and the afternoon siesta, among other time-honored traditions— were grudgingly giving way to business suits and agendas, tall hotels and shopping malls. But if you picked carefully, you could still thread the attenuated needle of yesterday, walk through streets in ancient, tattered neighborhoods, buy ice cream in a shady park, or drink hot coffee sitting in the sun and looking out to sea.

One or two days a month Barbara and I allowed ourselves the luxury of immersing our spirits in the timeless continuum of the city. Rising early we would visit libraries and specialty stores in the morning, then at noon relax over an extended lunch, just as every resident did, after prowling the Bairro Alto in search of the perfect bistro. We would hunt until we found a quiet dark corner of a restaurant with few tables where the waiters still wore long aprons and every meal was a minor festival. Then, drugged with heavy food and a warm feeling of complacency, we would trudge off to screenings of obscure art films at the Cinemateca or some embassy's cultural center. The day complete, and weary of the city's boisterousness, we would wend our way back to Mummy's apartment and the tranquillity of the countryside. It seemed a perfect blend of city and country—one always made you nostalgic for the other, and the other was never far away.

This particular day found us in Lisbon, and although planned as a workday at the cottage, we had quickly decided we needed a diversion. Things that week had taken a typically incongruent course early on. I had spent the day before madly rushing around the countryside negotiating for big trucks to deliver copious amounts of sand. I blamed myself for not having the materials ready for António's arrival and had vowed not to disgrace myself again. In an obvious attempt to counterbalance my act of omission, I had ordered literally tons of sand—river sand, white sand, red sand, yellow sand. One by one the trucks appeared, and their arrival quickly made me aware of another folly in my planning. It seemed that the lovely cobbled road that led down to our cottage was too narrow for even the smallest of the trucks to pass, and in a hastily arranged compromise, they dumped their contents at the top of the alley, attempting to pile the sand as carefully as possible against the low stucco walls of the little central square. At first unsure how to proceed, I decided to obtain the official cachet of *Senhor* Pimenta before committing some act that might draw the villagers' wrath down upon us. He had merely shrugged and said that our renovations would benefit everyone. Surely no one would object to a little sand in the streets.

Looking at the huge piles that now covered the alleyway completely, I tried to form in my mind a definition of what "a little" sand might be. What lay before me seemed more like the Sahara. That fact, coupled with the intensely inquisitive stares of the villagers, made me resolve to move this small desert closer to the house as soon as possible.

Unfortunately, we did not own the proper vehicle for moving sand—a wheelbarrow. I had balked at buying one. They were expensive and, I thought, would have limited uses. But as I stood contemplating the huge dunes, a villager walked by, assessed the situation, and without hesitation offered his assistance. An old wheelbarrow magically appeared along with a shovel. I began to load the wheelbarrow, noting unhappily the complete lack of impact my shovelsful seemed to have on the mounds of sand.

We decided that Barbara could take the wheelbarrow down the hill. Since the incline was fairly steep, it would require little strength. She had only to walk behind it and guide the wheel along its course. By the time the first load was ready, we had drawn a great deal of attention. People were gathered in the square, and it seemed all the windows of the village were open, filled with dark-eyed faces scrutinizing our every move.

Well, I thought, we would show them we weren't afraid to work, that we weren't like the other foreigners who hired others to do everything. I gave Barbara the signal, and she began her descent.

I realized my miscalculations immediately. Even though the total weight of the wheelbarrow was not that great, the incline of the alley was too much for Barbara. She lost control about halfway down the slope and screamed loudly for help. But before I could reach her, the wheelbarrow was careening wildly, dragging her behind it. I yelled for her to let go. It was too late. The wheelbarrow crashed through a thin wooden gate without stopping, scattering crazed chickens in its wake. Barbara finally let go, and together we watched the sand-laden missile splinter the front door of our neighbor's house.

There was a long silence after the "accident," punctuated only by the sound of windows closing. I looked around in embarrassment and noted that people were quickly disappearing from the square. In the opening where our neighbor's door had once stood a disheveled man appeared. Obviously awakened from a deep sleep, he looked curiously at the remnants of wood still hanging from the door's hinges. Then he disappeared for a moment and returned pushing the guilty wheelbarrow out through the doorway. He set it down gingerly in the yard.

After making sure that Barbara was all right, I picked up the little gate and tried to set it back in its frame. It teetered, then fell. We approached the man, and I began apologizing profusely. He seemed to listen, running his hands through his thick hair. There was the strong odor of alcohol in the air, and several chickens returned to the yard and began to peck at Barbara's pants legs.

And so it was that I baptized my shiny new tools by making extensive repairs on a neighbor's house. Fortunately, one of the doors from our cottage fit into the void with only minor alterations, and a few hours later the hastily assembled family finally approved the finished product. The door now had a fancy brass lockset in place of the strand of barbed wire that had once held it closed. The fresh paint glistened in the sunset. And our sand, coached by strong winds that appeared from nowhere, began to blow all over the village.

The next morning, before plotting our escape to Lisbon, we consorted with António. He arrived on time, shook my hand, and inquired about our escapade with the wheelbarrow. He found it immensely funny and even went to inspect the new door, reacting to its bright color with a loud whistle. Then, after gazing at the shifting mounds of sand, he carefully unpacked his tools from an oilcloth pouch.

"All right," he said, "what were we going to do today?" I took him into the first room of the dirt-floored ground level, the room in which we planned to locate the kitchen. We needed windows here, I explained. It was too dark.

António looked around calmly, surveying the contours of the room. He went to one of the many support posts, rapped it, and clucked his tongue. No, no, no, no, he repeated under his breath. It was too dangerous to work in this area. I asked him what he meant, and he directed me to stand in the doorway. Then, oblivious to my shouts, he proceeded to knock out several of the posts with his mason's hammer. There was a loud creaking, and suddenly part of the upper level came crashing down to the ground. Dust rose into the sky in a spiraling mushroom cloud. I coughed loudly as it filled my lungs. Antonio emerged dirty but grinning, slapping his hands together.

"I'll be back when you have this all cleaned up," he said. Then he climbed onto his mini-motorcycle and, working the engine hard, drove deftly through the drifts of sand.

It was just after the dust had settled that we decided to go to Lisbon. And now, sitting in a remote corner of an art deco café, we contemplated the initial disasters in our building careers. We spoke little, and when we did, it was only to comment on how much we disliked the Portuguese national dish. *Bacalhau,* or dried cod, we agreed, could never really be made elegant. Even though every restaurant proclaimed its version of bacalhau sublime, we found that the chunky fish rarely ventured beyond the threshold of edibility. Caught somewhere off Norway, air-dried and heavily coated with salt, bacalhau had somehow found its way into the exalted pantheon of Portuguese delicacies. It was a total mystery to us. There were so many succulent fresh fish available, it made no sense to spend time preparing these flat, rock-hard pieces from the Pleistocene era.

But the Portuguese ate bacalhau in great quantities. Almost every kitchen had a corner where the desiccated slabs were set aside to revive in a large pan of water, and several days later chunks of cod would appear in casseroles and fricassees, stews and soufflés. The variations seemed endless, and we had made it our personal crusade to find at least one rendition that might be palatable. So far we had been unsuccessful, but we vowed to continue the quest.

Today's recipe was a cream-based affair with big lumps of cod hidden among overdone potato wedges and smothered in a thick, lemon-scented white sauce. It needed garlic, we agreed, and capers. And a touch of wine perhaps, along with some fresh herbs. But most of all, we concurred, it needed another fish, preferably a fresh one rather than this coarse, sinewy, resurrected salt lick.

Nevertheless, we were very thankful. We were warm, dry, and well fed. We had escaped the morning's calamities unscathed, with only a residue of dust clogging our noses and a few grains of sand in our shoes. True, our renovation schedule had suffered a grievous blow along with our budget, but there was wine on the table, and an air of conviviality flowed through the café.

•

WE MADE THE MOST OF OUR MORNING WITH A VISIT TO AN ARCHITECtural salvage yard in Lisbon. Sara had given us directions, assuring us that the yard contained countless treasures that would suit the cottage perfectly. We got lost, of course, but finally located the

yard not too far from the airport. It was a grand collection of statues and columns, tiles and roof beams. The proprietor was a little
round man in a dirty beret who guided us with unrestrained glee
through room after room of what he called "objets d'art," all out-
rageously priced. There was everything here to decorate a house
in any style imaginable. Unfortunately we saw nothing to *build* a
house with. But the little round man would not take no for an
answer. Insisting that his prices were the "best in Iberia," he
forced us to look at huge marble fountains, Corinthian columns
as high as a tree, and gargantuan entry doors made of exotic
woods.

I told him that we were on a budget, the "smallest in
Iberia," and that the house we were renovating was rustic and
simple—not a palace that required the items he was showing
us. Finally, with a shrug, he gave up, obviously judging us to be
intractable and inscrutable. He retreated to the tiny cubicle that
was his office and closed the door.

That was fine because it allowed us the freedom to roam
around outside at our own pace. And it took only a few minutes
to find a totally unique necessity—a beautiful cast-iron spiral
staircase that lay in pieces scattered among sections of wrought-
iron railings. We needed an interior staircase to link the two
floors of the cottage and quickly realized that this would be perfect. I counted the sections. There were enough for our needs
plus one or two extra.

Out of the corner of my eye I saw the proprietor emerge
from his office and head in our direction. Had he noticed our
interest in the staircase? Hopefully not, as it would put a crimp
in our bargaining capabilities. I hastily put down the section of
staircase I had in my hand and gave it a rude kick for good measure.

But our interest had not gone unnoticed. The proprietor
approached us with a large smile on his face. *"Então, o senhor
gosta disto?"*

"Oh, no, not at all," I said, shaking my head emphatically.

"Oh, yes," Barbara said. *"Quanto custa?"*

I shuddered and contemplated strangling her on the spot. Not only had she revealed our interest, she had asked the price. Negotiating would be difficult if not impossible now. I had learned long ago that to get the best price you had to feign total lack of interest in the object you wanted. Disdain it, hate it, then convince the seller that you were doing him a favor by taking it off his hands.

It was too late for all that now. The man doffed his cap and began pulling out the pieces of the staircase from among the iron railings. He brought one of the ornate steps over to Barbara and held it up to her.

"It's a miracle, isn't it? Look how beautiful!"

I tried to intercept, grabbing the piece. "Look how rusty!" I said, rubbing the dirt on my fingers for effect.

"Ah," the man countered. "That is because it's very old."

"Not so old," I said. "Not old enough to have value."

"Then it's new!" he said. "It has to be one or the other."

As I calculated my response, the man directed his attention to Barbara. "This," he said, pointing to the ornate iron work, "this is quality. Look closely, madame. These things are not made like this anymore."

I replied that certainly they were still made. In fact, we had already seen several other versions this morning—clean staircases that had not been left out in the rain to rust.

But the man continued to plug away at Barbara who smiled and nodded her head, not understanding half of what he was saying.

"This is from the Salazar Palace," he said with emphasis.

"There is no Salazar Palace," I responded.

"But if there was one, this staircase would have been there."

We all laughed and retrenched for the next round. Barbara tried to get my attention by whispering under her breath, "I love it. We have to get it."

I pinched her, hoping she would get the message. The little man was ordering the treads and risers into a neat pile.

"So," I began again, "even though we can't really use this, we were wondering how much it might cost."

"Did *Dona* Sara send you?" he asked.

"Yes," I said, not thinking. "I mean no, no."

"Yes, she did," the man said gleefully, tweaking his beret with his fingers. "I have to give her a percentage of the price, you know."

I hadn't considered this at all. No wonder Sara had extolled the virtues of this junkyard. She was in for a piece of the pie.

"A percentage?" I asked. "A percentage of what price?"

The man looked down at the ground. "Maybe three hundred thousand."

"What!" I hoped my tone of voice indicated the extent of my surprise.

"That would be clean, of course. I would clean it up," he said, pawing at the ground with his shoe.

"And what if *we* were to clean it? What then?"

"Maybe the same price. Maybe a little less."

"How much less?"

He looked up at me. "Two hundred fifty thousand?"

"Outrageous!" I grabbed Barbara by the arm and turned her toward the car. Not expecting this, she let out a loud gasp. Perfect effect, I thought, as we marched off in feigned indignation.

But the little man caught up with us and held up a hand to stop us. "Look," he said. "Maybe we can do something about this—if you don't need a receipt and we keep it off the record."

He winked at me several times to make his point. What he referred to was the practice of selling goods without paying government taxes. Everybody did it, and I was certain that no matter what the price, he wasn't about to pay the tax anyway. But it opened up the road to further negotiations.

"Okay," I said. "How much off the record?"

"Two hundred thousand," he said. "My wife will beat me and my children will starve, but I must be polite to foreigners." He went on to mention what a steal it would be at that price. He would be selling it for less than he had paid for it. But business was business, and sometimes you had to take a loss to satisfy a customer.

I listened patiently until he was finished. "Well then," I said, "if that's the price off the record, we might as well keep it off the record and not even tell Sara we bought it here. How much would it be then?"

This upset him a little. He made several gruff sounds and slapped his cap on his leg. Then he began another discourse about how Sara sent him a lot of business and that she would surely find out what we had done. The country of Portugal was like a very small village, and sooner or later everyone found out about everything, he said.

I said fine. If that was the case, it was better that we not buy anything. Otherwise, people would find out that we had paid a high price for the staircase and would expect us to pay a high price for everything.

We started for the car again, but he cut us off. "Shhhh," he said, putting a finger to his lips to indicate silence. "One hundred fifty thousand. No word to Sara. Shhhh."

I explained to Barbara what was going on, and she reaffirmed her desire to buy the staircase. The price was getting better, I thought. I had no idea of the relative value of the piece, but neither did the little man. It was obvious that the staircase had been lying around for a decade or two. That, coupled with the rampant rate of inflation, left us dealing in a vague netherworld of commas and zeros, all of which had little bearing on reality.

I was tiring, so I accepted the little man's last offer. He called his minions eagerly, almost too eagerly, I thought. I, meanwhile, backed up the van, and we loaded the staircase on carefully, wiping the major dirt off each piece as we went. Once everything was in, I counted the pieces, then resolved to attempt one last bargaining maneuver.

"There's one piece missing," I said.

The little man seemed surprised. "What? That's not possible."

"Look," I said, "there are thirteen risers but only twelve treads."

He took off his beret and began counting. I crossed my fingers, hoping that he didn't know much about the building trades. There was always an extra riser, of course, since the upstairs landing took the place of a tread.

I saw a look of concern spread over the little man's face as he finished counting and commanded his men to search the lot for the missing piece. I pretended to be equally concerned and joined in the search. A few minutes later we gave up. The missing tread was nowhere to be found. We exchanged shrugs and a few vague words, and I began to unload the pieces slowly.

The little man paced back and forth behind the van. "You can't use it at all?" he asked plaintively.

"No," I replied.

But surely, he said, we could shorten the house by simply lowering the roof a few centimeters. Then the staircase would work, he was sure of it.

I said that might be possible, but even if it were, it would be very expensive. We couldn't afford to buy the staircase if we were going to alter the house in such a radical manner.

"All right, all right," he said, wringing his hands. "One hundred thousand."

•

LATER, AT THE RESTAURANT, BARBARA AND I TOASTED OUR ACQUISITION. It was a beautiful piece of artwork, and with minimal labor the staircase would be a grand centerpiece for the living room. It was the first time I had ever really been successful at bargaining. Sara's influence perhaps? I contemplated my future in the marketplace. And how would it look on my résumé?

We finally relinquished our table, paid our check, and wandered out into the afternoon sunlight. The narrow alleys of the Bairro Alto were alive with motion as people and vehicles fought for control of the thin strip of cobblestones that ran between the jumbled buildings. The sun played on the roofs of the ancient plastered dwellings, spilling over onto balconies and terraces, creating a chiaroscuro effect and highlighting the endless rows of drying laundry that stretched away into the distance.

It was as if centuries had melted away. We peered into tiny dimly lit shops where old men hunched over worn tables, performing obscure tasks with gold leaf, leather, or filigree. There were art galleries, antique stores, then, incongruously, boutiques displaying the latest in Italian interior design furnishings. Punctuating all this were the requisite bars and cafés with exotic names—the High Heel, Pastor's Pasture, Fragile. It all seemed to be part of a vast continuum of life here—playful, eclectic, eternal. And we would soon become a part of it, immersing ourselves in this colorful spectrum of the senses—if only the renovation would move along quickly.

Daily Rituals

13 THREE DAYS LATER WE FI-
nally removed the last splintered debris and rubble from the
ground floor. It was an eerie sensation, standing on the dirt
floor and gazing up at the upper floor's ceiling high above us.
But I had to admit that in the end António was probably right.
The wooden floor and the joists were totally rotten. They
crumbled into dust when we touched them, and ugly, wood-

boring insects emerged and wriggled pitifully in the sunlight.

Even though we felt we had accomplished absolutely nothing, a huge pile of debris had already accumulated just off to the side of the little cottage. I hadn't really planned for its disposal, and the fact that vehicles could not pass through the narrow alley somewhat concerned me. But, I thought, surely António would have an idea.

Just as we finished dumping the last wheelbarrow load of debris onto the pile, António arrived. We had come to recognize the sound of his motorcycle engine, laboring under the stress of transporting him. As always a cigarette dangled from his lips, and I was in admiration of his ability to smoke while piloting his noisy machine.

He dismounted and looked at the pile of rubble, whistling and shaking his head. *"Isto vai ser um problema,"* he said.

Yes, I responded, it did seem to be a growing problem.

"Well, as long as we've gone this far," António said, "we might as well tear down the whole thing and start all over."

I protested, citing the historical value of the house.

António held up his hand. "I'm only joking," he said. "There's lots more work for me fixing this thing up. Months, maybe years."

I hoped his estimate was a joke, too. I scanned his face for obvious signs of levity. There were none.

"All right," he said. "Let's go to work."

We went inside and stared at the thick white walls just as we had done several days before. "Windows here?" António asked.

I nodded.

"Well, put a mark up where you want them."

I was prepared for this. Barbara and I had examined the walls carefully, planning the positions of the several windows we wanted to add. It was important to locate them properly in order not to jeopardize the harmony of the facade. It would also be difficult to correct mistakes in three-foot-thick walls.

I went to the wall and with a heavy pencil reinforced the outlines I had traced several days earlier. Without hesitation, António picked up a chisel and a round-headed hammer and attacked the wall, grunting with each strike. His blows were phenomenally forceful. The entire house seemed to shake. Layers of plaster fell to the ground around him, and in a few minutes the rubble masonry of the wall was exposed. Now we were making progress!

Barbara and I stood and watched in awe as António whacked away vigorously. It was only after he had pulled several large rocks from the wall that I stopped him. "António," I began, not quite sure how to phrase my question. "Aren't you concerned that the wall might fall if you pull all those stones out?"

He frowned. "No, why?"

And if the wall fell, I said, then the roof might go with it.

He nodded in agreement. "So?"

Somewhat perplexed, I remarked that the roof falling might not be a pretty thing. It would make the project much more expensive and certainly add several more tons to our debris pile.

António put his arm around me and pulled me close to the wall. "You see those stones?" he asked.

Yes, I responded.

"Those stones have been there three hundred years at least, right?"

I agreed.

"Well, you know how you feel when you lie down and watch television for a few hours. You get into a certain position and it hurts to change."

Okay, I agreed.

"Well," he continued, "these stones have been in the same position for three hundred years, so they don't want to change, either. Right?"

I would have to think about that, I replied.

"Think about all the earthquakes. Look." He loosened

some of the packing from the wall. "You see this? This isn't mortar. It's just mud. That's all they had in the past, but it worked. The 1755 earthquake destroyed Lisbon, but it didn't hurt this wall. Mud lets the stones grind together, like this."

He showed me his tiny little teeth and ground them together to illustrate his point. "You see?"

Barbara and I were both very impressed by the entire demonstration, and we said so.

"Other than that," António concluded, "it's all in God's hands. If the roof wants to fall, it will fall. It doesn't look very good to me anyway. So. Come on, it's time for a break."

He led us out through the garden and gate, over the narrow alleyway, then down the path in front of the little chapel, an architectural gem with its pillared portico and curving roof line. Farther down the path we rounded a corner and entered a cavernous hole-in-the-wall. Inside this dark dungeon were several tables and chairs. Toward the rear was a bar of sorts and behind that the oldest refrigerator I had ever seen.

Barbara tugged on my shirt sleeve. "You see?" she said. "This is the café I told you about."

"Great," I responded, noting the dirty walls and peeling plaster. "Maybe they have a postcard we can send to friends."

I felt a prodding at my back. *Dona* China was sitting at a table in a corner, poking me with her cane.

"*Dona* China," I said, happy to see her. She was not only our next-door neighbor, we had discovered, but our houses shared a common wall.

"Well, are you going to buy me a drink or not?" she demanded.

Yes, of course, I replied. António and the bartender were watching us. I said that China had asked for a drink, and the bartender, a small, skinny man with a huge mustache, yelled over to her, asking her what she wanted.

"Nothing," she responded. "I don't want anything except a

man. I was just testing him. But put something on his tab. I may want a drink tomorrow."

I laughed and brought Barbara over to her table to introduce them.

"I know who she is," China said. "She's the woman you'll have to leave to marry me."

I translated for Barbara who held out her hand. China took it and shook it briskly. "Excuse me for not getting up," she said. "I only have energy to get up for the king and queen, and they're dead, I think."

She continued to hold Barbara's hand, then examined her fingers. "You bite your nails, I see. You know what that means."

Barbara pulled back her hand in embarrassment, and China poked me again with her cane. "You," she said, "you're not keeping her busy enough at night. That's the problem. Ha ha!"

António motioned me back to the bar and introduced me to the bartender. "José," he said.

I offered my hand and José took it, shaking it vigorously. *"Muito prazer,"* he said, his face breaking into a broad smile. "And welcome to Eugaria."

António patted me on the back and drew my attention to the line of bottles displayed on a shelf behind the bar. They all contained national brands, liquors I had never seen before. My eyes wandered over the bottles and then down to the plastic tub that served as the wash-up receptacle. It was full of dirty water. I saw thick layers of film on the glasses that stood on the bar and suddenly realized there was no running water—the bane of the village.

António pressed me to make a selection. *"Um café se faz favor,"* I said in my most polite tone.

"No," António said. "With your coffee what do you want?"

I said that I was unfamiliar with the different brands.

"Time to change that," António declared and proceeded to reel off several names. José obliged by setting down several glasses of different shapes and deftly filling them to the brim with exotic-colored liquids.

Barbara had finally escaped China and now joined us at the bar. "What's all this?" she asked looking down at the motley collection of glasses and potions. "Chemistry one-o-one?"

I gave Barbara a false smile. "I think I'm supposed to drink all this."

"Perfect," she said. "Then do what? Have your stomach pumped?"

António lifted the glass on his far right; then bending back what little neck he had, he threw its contents down his throat. He closed his eyes, shook his head, let out a long, low sigh of relief, and slammed the glass back down on the bar.

He pointed to another glass on the bar and announced its contents, *"Amêndoa amarga. Experimenta!"*

I picked up the glass and braced my palette for impact. I had never heard of a drink called Bitter Almond and couldn't imagine how it might taste. Staring down into the thick gold liquid, I was sure I saw microbes doing the breast stroke. But there seemed to be no polite way out of the situation, so, closing my eyes, I lifted the glass and drank. It was sticky and sweet, heavily perfumed with the essence of almond. I swallowed slowly, nodding my head in mock approval, then watched as José refilled António's glass.

"Well?" António asked, slapping me on the back.

"Excellent," I said. "Very good."

"Try the next one," António urged. "Licor Beirão."

I tried the next one. It was sweet, acidic, and orangy. Then, hoping to stem the tide, I ordered coffees and asked António if he would like one.

"Oh, no," he said, downing a second glass of a liquid that was distinctly yellow. "Coffee's bad for your teeth."

And so António's first day of labor proceeded as our morning break edged into lunchtime at the dirty little bar. We did succeed, however, in opening an official account. José celebrated by bringing out an entire new ledger, dedicating several hundred pages, it seemed, for our exclusive use. We would be here often, he told us. There was another bar in the village, but it was open only sporadically. His bar was always open, and we would have to come here to pass the periods of rain and cold.

Lunchtime came officially, and magically the bar began to fill up with people and stray dogs that wandered in off the street. The television, stuck away in a corner, was turned on with great pomp and circumstance. José took pleasure in introducing us to all who arrived, giving us elaborate explanations of everyone's lineage followed by descriptions of which house he lived in. It was hopeless to try to follow either discourse. We merely smiled and nodded. Several people tried to buy us drinks, but we declined. I was already feeling unstable, and Barbara, well, she was trying hard to be invisible.

António had excused himself for lunch, saying that he was going home to eat. He would be back in an hour. We didn't see him again for three days.

Work in Progress

14

A FEW WEEKS LATER WE Finally had a routine established. I arrived at the cottage around seven, opened up all the doors, then arranged the materials we were going to need that day. If I had time, I took the wheelbarrow we had finally purchased down to the old spring. There, dipping into the small trough bucket by bucket, I filled the large plastic barrel that rode on the wheelbarrow. This would be our water supply for the morning.

Around eight António would arrive—unless, of course, he didn't. We had had a long discussion weeks before about his attendance. I had tried to impress upon him my very American-oriented views regarding reliability and punctuality. He appeared to be a serious audience, repeating his vow that he intended to come to work every day. And when he failed to appear, he selected and proffered from among his vast repertory of excuses whichever one he thought most likely to fit the circumstances. There were potato plantings, vine prunings, grape sprayings, mushroom hunts, and a long series of deaths among distant relatives whose exact relationship António could not recall.

He was also a volunteer fireman, he had told us, and true enough, he would disappear sometimes when the siren went off. Eventually I learned to read the blips and bleeps of the siren and realized that António was using the alarms as an excuse to vanish into the nearest bar. I thought it would be socially remiss of me to call his bluff, so I did the next best thing. I joined the fire department. For several weeks every time the alarm sounded, I would stop whatever I was doing and ask António if we had to go, knowing full well it was only the noon whistle. António would invariably say no, it was just a test.

I did ask him once about weekends. Why was it he never sprayed grapes on the weekends? He looked very surprised and responded that grapes were always sprayed during the week. Weekends were for fishing or drinking and nothing else.

As António's pattern of absence became more methodical, I came to understand and define the intrinsic motivation of the Portuguese worker. To begin with, the most important factor was life. Nothing was to be missed, be it a birth, wedding, death, or some other important event—"other" including a vast nebula of circumstances, including baby's first steps, soccer games, even installments of certain soap operas. All took precedence over "professional" life, relegating work to the category of things that one "might" do should absolutely no other option present itself that day. As António frequently pointed out, work could always wait. There was absolutely nothing in the world that could not be done tomorrow or next week. He told me not to worry about the July deadline. Everything would work out even though, he admitted, the project would be far from done.

In the beginning I rebelled against this philosophy. But I gradually came to see my work ethic as something engendered in me by my upbringing, something taught and reinforced over the years. And as I reviewed these firmly entrenched beliefs, I realized that in the end they were no more valid than those I chastised António for having.

Nor did economic considerations seem to carry much weight. Although in America one might have to work in order to eat, in Portugal the situation was quite different. Every individual had a vast network of family he could call upon in times of need. There was always an uncle in the Alentejo with a pig farm who showed up sporadically to distribute pork rations. Or just as likely a brother or son in France who sent home monthly stipends to be disbursed to the family. Although it was technically a poor country, it seemed that in Portugal no one really needed to work in order to survive. One worked because at times there was simply nothing else to do.

On the other hand, working too much was frowned upon. Being assertive and aggressive was considered bad form, and any attempt to move ahead in the world was considered an affront to the will of God. It was a fatalistic society: one's destiny was determined by a random series of events, the "ricochets" of reality, totally sporadic and unpredictable. And so we now ascribed António's appearances or disappearances to fate. But to counterbalance fate, if that was at all possible, we did something else—we hired another *pedreiro*. Paulo was a cousin of António's who had shown up one day and indicated his availability. António wanted to hire him on the spot. Still concerned about our budget then, we had said no, we would wait and see how things were going. Now we rationalized that if Paulo's work habits paralleled António's, it would really cost no more since they would both take multiple days off.

Barbara's routine was somewhat more problematic. The first few days she had attempted to get up with me and be at the site early. But by nature she was a late-night person, and the morning hours usually found her response bordering on the catatonic. Tasks she attempted rarely turned out the way they should. She had already ignited several fires by trying to remove paint with a torch too close to mineral spirits. So we had decided that she would come later in the morning, hopefully bringing lunch with her. This was successful at first until she caught on to António's philosophy, which she readily adopted as her own. Each day she came later, and she, too, had a repertory of excuses. She was teaching Mathias, one of the young "masons" we had interviewed, how to paint. He had problems with drugs and alcohol, and she thought it would be good therapy for him. Or she had letters to write or clothes to wash, or she hadn't slept well or her arms were sore. Or, best of all, she had seen António in the bar and assumed we had stopped working for the day.

Thus, the routine was sometimes a lonely one. I looked forward to Paulo's arrival, perhaps within a few days. All things considered, however, the project moved along at a steady pace. We had managed to create several openings for windows, which was exciting. It was the first time natural light had entered the ground floor of the cottage in over three hundred years.

I wanted to forge ahead with the window project but immediately encountered a formidable hurdle. It was just after we had set reinforced concrete lintels over the openings that António asked where the *cantarias* were. I didn't recognize the word, so he explained that they were the traditional cut-stone frames that went around the window openings. I nodded, then, as had become habit, prepared myself for the drive down to the hardware store.

António laughed and told me not to bother. *Cantarias,* he said, were two hundred to three hundred years old and not a hardware store item. Where could we get them then, I asked. We couldn't finish the new windows without them. The old windows had stone frames, so we would have to find something to match.

António thought for a moment, then declared that he knew where several might be found. Leaping onto his motorcycle, he took off in a cloud of dust. We didn't see him again for two days.

In addition to the window openings, we also managed to create a new upper floor to replace the part of the old one that had collapsed. Utilizing reinforced concrete beams and special tile insets as a base, we poured a concrete floor. A simple and expedient system, it was the way most floors were being constructed in our area. Although we had not wanted to use modern materials, we knew we would be able to disguise the concrete with a few coats of stucco on the lower ceiling and terra-cotta pavers on the new floor itself. The part of the second floor that had not collapsed was structurally sound, and we had decided to leave it in its rustic state—peeled chestnut logs supporting pine flooring.

•

ALTHOUGH PROGRESS HAD ITS REWARDS, IT ALSO HAD ITS DRAW-backs. The more money and labor we poured into the house, the more we became concerned about ultimate ownership. The cogs of bureaucracy were turning slowly, and still no date for the closing had been set. This made us very uneasy since the owners could repossess at any time merely by refunding our deposit. And we hesitated to increase the deposit because there was no guarantee that we would be allowed to purchase the property. The government was very fickle in enforcing its laws concerning property purchases by foreigners—probably because no one knew what the laws were. Sara had summed it up succinctly: "In the end, if they like you, they let you buy."

With this in mind we calculated our costs carefully. We wanted to tip the balance of expenditures toward the end of the project when we would have the deed in hand and thereby be assured of ownership. But we were quickly reaching a point where money would have to start to flow freely. Doors, windows, plumbing fixtures—all these were expensive items.

I had made the many requisite trips to government agencies. I had gone to a bank in Lisbon to request permission to import funds to buy property. Twice I had met with immigration officials in Cascais to petition for residency. A resident was exempt from the hefty SISA, or transfer tax, of 12 percent. I had visited the *notários* office in Sintra to update the tattered deed we had been given and, most time-consuming of all, spent several hours in line at the "finance office" to receive a fiscal number and file for a myriad of exemptions for reasons no one seemed to understand.

But still we waited for the necessary licenses, permits, and other documents to appear, revisiting each office at intervals to try to discover what might be causing the delay. There was never any rational reason. It just took an eternity for the papers to be passed from desk to desk, to acquire this or that stamp, or for arcane numbers to be entered in dusty ledgers.

But if at times we suffered from bureaucratic neurosis, the villagers proved to be a continual source of delight. Most would drop by daily to offer advice and criticism. Some regaled us with stories of former residents or of the village itself. China dropped in every few hours to remind us that our cottage and hers had once been a single dwelling until the two sisters who owned it had had an argument and subsequently divided it. She joked that she wanted it to become one house again so we could heat her bedroom and she would have a functioning indoor toilet instead of having to go out to the garden. We assumed she was exaggerating until one day we observed her over the fallen stone wall. What we had thought was a storage shed was in reality a rickety outhouse.

China came by one day, dressed in her multiple layers of scarves, and reenacted an accident that had occurred at the cottage twenty years ago. Mounting the outdoor staircase to the little second-floor porch, she proceeded to demonstrate how the former tenant, a cousin of hers, had slipped on one of the steps and fell to her death, banging her head this way and that. China was very animated, indicating with her cane exactly where the poor woman's head had struck and how she had staggered, injured, in the garden. She pointed to a spot near the nêspera tree and informed us that this was where the villagers had found the poor woman. After that, she claimed, the nêspera tree began to bear more fruit than any other.

Besides rampant absenteeism and escalating costs, there had been few other complications with the project. True, we had arrived one day to find all our tools gone, but António came up with an immediate solution. Striding into the bar, he made a public announcement in a loud voice. The purloined tools were his, he said, and there would be trouble unless they reappeared within ten minutes.

It was only seven minutes later that João Ladrão appeared at the cottage carrying a large sack, apologizing profusely. "Oh, António, I didn't know these tools were yours. I saw them just sitting on a ledge in the house and thought that I should collect them just in case a thief might come by and steal them. They were safe at my house. I was just about to return them this morning."

I watched as António drew back his arm to strike him. João dropped the bag, cowered in a corner, and began to whimper. I moved forward to stop António, but he had already relaxed his fist. He yelled at João, called him several words I didn't recognize, and told him that he would henceforth be responsible for all our tools for the duration of the project. If anything happened to them, even if one trowel was missing, he was going to hold João personally responsible. Did he understand?

João stood up, wiped his eyes, and replied that he understood. He would watch the house to make sure that no one bothered our things.

"Now go away!" António bellowed at him. And as João raced around the corner, António winked at me. "Now we have a guard for the house. And cheap." António must have noticed my look of concern. "Don't worry," he said. "I can't hit him. He's a cousin."

The next day a cement mixer appeared. There had been no announcement of its imminent arrival. It was just there that morning. I knew that cement mixers existed in Portugal, but throughout my travels I had never seen one in use. Up to this point we had been mixing mortar and cement on the ground. It was strenuous, very strenuous, but I had come to view it as a form of aerobic exercise and had more or less made peace with the process.

António arrived a few minutes later. After he had dismounted and parked his noisy machine, I asked him about the cement mixer. "For us?"

Yes, he replied.

"We're moving into the twentieth century?"

"We have to," he said.

"Oh?"

"People are talking. They think you are working too hard. And as the *patrão,* you shouldn't be mixing mortar."

I thought this notion odd and told António so. I really didn't mind mixing mortar.

"Well," António said, lighting up a cigarette, "they think if you work too hard, you'll become tired and want to stop the project."

"They?" I asked.

António didn't seem to hear. "Or," he continued, "you might have a heart attack and drop! And if that happens, the project stops, too. No more work for anyone."

I protested that I was in perfect health, didn't smoke, and even began to detail my diet when António interrupted. "The other problem is honor," he said. "It's not honorable for the *patrão* to perform the duties of a *servente*."

That was it then. The villagers were giving António a bad time, thinking that he was forcing me to work too hard. Whether it was due to his absences or the fact that I was a foreigner, I decided not to press the issue. The cement mixer would certainly speed the process and save us both labor. I told António I thought it was a good idea.

"There's one other thing," he said. "You have to rent it."

I expressed surprise and asked whom it belonged to.

"It's mine," he said. "But it's the tradition that the *patrão* always rents the mixer—one thousand escudos per day."

I calculated quickly. In three months that would equal the price of three new mixers! I pointed this out to António, asking if the rent had to be paid on those days he didn't show up.

He laughed and said of course. But, he added, Paulo was starting next week, and he would come every day.

I began to protest again, but he stopped me short. He thought I would object, so he had come up with a solution. Instead of paying rent for the mixer during the remainder of the project, I need only buy him and Paulo a present. Not a present, really, but a tool. A tool we would need for the project. We would use the tool, and then at the end of the project, they would keep it. Simple, he said.

I asked what tool he had in mind.

"A chain saw," he replied.

"I see. How much does that cost?"

"Forty-five thousand."

"Hmmmm."

"We might be able to get it for forty thousand at the co-op."

"Did you and Paulo come up with this idea?"

"Yes," António said. "But it took a lot of *bagaço*."

Bagaço was the generic word for *grappa*. It was clear, cheap, and incredibly potent. I was glad I had missed that meeting. Forty-five thousand was certainly less than the accumulated rent might be on the mixer, but I was still chagrined by the element of blackmail inherent in his proposal. When I mentioned that to António, he merely shrugged. I finally came up with an idea of my own.

"No problem," I said. "We'll do it your way as long as the project is done by July 1."

António's eyes opened wide. "No way!" he said. "That's too much work!"

"But Paulo's coming, and he's going to work every day," I reminded him.

True enough, António admitted. But soon it would be spring and the heavy rains would come. Not to mention hunting season. He went on to list a few dozen other reasons, and I saw that he had enough excuses never to work another day of his life.

But, António said, since he liked us and didn't want any hard feelings, he would make us a deal. If by the end of the project I could lift the cement mixer alone, then we could keep the chain saw.

I looked over at the mixer. It was old and appeared very heavy. There were bits of hardened mortar sticking to the blades in the drum, and the wheels were encrusted in mud.

"Lift the cement mixer?" I asked. "Alone?"

"Right," António said. "It's not so bad. I can do it."

I looked again at the mixer and then at António. His challenge had struck the right chord. I felt my pride rise up inside me. Poor *patrão,* too tired to mix mortar. We would see. I could lift the mixer, I was sure of it. I walked over to it and tapped its steel frame. It made a heavy, solid sound.

"Agreed," I said and extended my hand.

António shook it, a very mischievous look on his face.

Stone Cottage

15

ONE DAY *Senhor* José and *Dona* Lucinda invited us to visit their house. A couple in their eighties, they lived down the dirt pathway that passed in front of the cottage. "Just beyond the old spring," they always told us, pointing in that direction. It was here that the boundaries of their property began, framed by huge plane trees and a crude whitewashed wooden portal.

Since the path in front of the cottage was the only access to their domain, José and Lucinda passed frequently, always bearing kind words and encouragement. Lucinda was very excited to have new neighbors, especially, she commented, "young people who would animate the village." She had been born in the little white house whose roof we could see down the pathway. And she had lived there ever since, only "allowing," as she put it, José to move in after they had married seventy-three years ago.

We loved them especially for their mode of dress—always formal, always pressed, always turn-of-the-century. José wore pleated trousers, a white dress shirt with vest and pocket watch, and a fedora that he invariably tipped to us as he ambled past. Lucinda was much more conservative and dressed in layers of underskirts and overskirts in such a profusion that we could never figure out where they began and ended. Their house had always intrigued us. There seemed to be no water or electricity hookups of any kind. We asked them how they had gotten by all these years. We would have to come and see, they told us each time we inquired, and today was the day.

They collected us just after completing their daily shopping at *Senhor* Pimenta's store. Barbara and I each took a bag to assist them, and together we made our way down the hard earth path. I marveled that all the building materials for their house had passed down this same narrow trail. José looked at me from under the brim of his hat. "Donkeys," he said. "Donkeys carried it all."

When we reached the fragile little gate, José proudly took a large key from his vest pocket and inserted it in the gate's keyhole. As he turned it he announced, "I changed this lock last in 1927."

The gate creaked open, and we entered what seemed to be a different world. Most noticeable and not at all visible from our cottage were the extensive gardens that lay in little terraces all around the house, each apparently designated for a different type of plant or crop. There was cabbage, of course, several varieties interspersed among tiny plots of lettuce and kale. In another spot near the house, green onions grew wild, mingling with ponderous beets. There was also a profusion of flowers, cascading down the gentle embankment to the little stream that separated our property from theirs. Up close to the house was a proliferation of multicolored roses, many in full bloom.

We walked down a few steps and José stopped us. "Water," he said and tapped the ground where we stood. I looked around but saw nothing. Noticing my incomprehension, José elaborated. "A spring. Just here." He pointed to several clumps of moss. "It collects here," he said, indicating a small circular concrete slab set into the ground. "Open it up."

I found a tiny indentation in the concrete, enough to put a finger into, and I was able to pull the slab away from the earth. Underneath there was certainly water, a large cistern full. The daylight reflected our images on its surface. Sticking my hand down into the pool, I was surprised at how cold it was. I couldn't reach the bottom.

José told us that the house had been built here because they had found this spring. "Water is very important to the Portuguese," he said. Many people believed certain spirits lived in water, he added, spirits that would help the body fight disease and insanity. This water was especially good for the spleen.

I recounted my adventures with the water company, and they both shook their heads. Be careful, they warned. It was all politics, and the only way to get them to act was to embarrass them. When I mentioned the company's plan to locate a large holding tank up on the hill, José and Lucinda shook their heads again. That was an old plan, a plan and promise from several years ago. They were convinced the water company would do nothing. And why should it? Eugaria was just a tiny village full of poor people. Why would the water company bother? No one in the village had enough money for a decent bribe.

I purposely neglected to translate this last bit of information for Barbara and quickly changed the subject.

We walked down past the house and out to the point of land that surrounded it. Here the hillside sloped precariously, buttressed by intermittent boulders and a thick webbing of undergrowth. It was their own peninsula, José said, and, with the gate, their own private island. The views were wonderful. The sea was on the horizon to the west and on the other side stood the village, isolated and at an angle we had not yet seen. Its contours were very pleasant from this vantage point. It seemed to roll and bend comfortably over the hillside. Barbara pointed out our cottage. It was the first time we had seen it with the new openings for the windows. It seemed well balanced, but then again it was difficult to tell because of the increasing mass of debris piled next to it. In fact, the cottage seemed quite small.

After a brief tour of the gardens, José and Lucinda ushered us into their kitchen. It was like walking into a museum. There was an open-hearth fireplace; we had seen many of these, but never one complete with hanging cauldrons and glowing embers. She was still canning vegetables, Lucinda explained, and showed us her pantry. There were hundreds of glass jars of varying colors lined up neatly in rows across the back wall of the kitchen. Above them hung a profusion of drying herbs, their smells mingling with the essence of the wood smoke.

A simple farmer's table occupied the center of the room, covered by an elaborate handmade lace doily. On top of the doily was an oil lamp. I looked around but saw no other source of light. Was this it then? I asked José. Was this lamp their only light? José shook his head. Of course not, he said. He had another lamp in the bedroom. But no electricity? He shook his head again. No, he said, no electricity. They lived a simple life and had no use for it. It might be nice to have a refrigerator, but they had preserves instead. They once had had something that needed to be refrigerated—José couldn't remember what it was—but they had left it with *Senhor* Pimenta. He had a refrigerator. And television—well, if they really wanted to watch it, they could walk to the bar. They had a radio with batteries to keep up with the news. No, electricity was not missed. Besides, José warned me, it didn't pay to trust the electric company. They were bigger communists than the telephone company!

Were we going to have electricity, Lucinda asked. Probably we were, she thought. Young people had different needs.

They showed us their bedroom, a small chamber with whitewashed walls and an old, carved, country-style bed made up with snow-white sheets and covered by a heavy comforter. The walls were unadorned with the exception of a single mirror that hung at the far end of the room. The bathroom, too, was simple—a toilet with a bucket next to it for flushing and a forged iron washstand with a round ceramic bowl supported in its center. There was a white tin pitcher next to the stand, obviously for filling it. An old claw-foot bathtub completed the ensemble.

I remarked on the elegance of the tub's lines and the intricacy of the cast-iron feet. It was a wedding present, José told us. The family thought that if they remained clean, they would remain happy. So far, he said with a smile, it had worked.

•

I SPENT THE REST OF THE DAY CRUISING THE COUNTRYSIDE IN SEARCH of *cantarias*. All the people I questioned seemed to remember they knew someone with a pair of them lying in his front yard. Further investigation, usually involving several hours of driving, inevitably proved their memory to be faulty. No *cantarias* were to be found at Uncle Pedro's or Cousin Helena's house. But our arrival at these places was always met with courtesy and further enticing hints about where the elusive stones might be located.

I finally took a more pragmatic approach and drove to a number of marble quarries in the area. Surely companies that produced world-class marble would be able to throw together a couple of crude stone window frames, I thought. But I was wrong. No one lacked the expertise, it seemed. It was just that the particular type of stone from which *cantarias* were made no longer existed. If I could find a few tons of this stone, they told me, then certainly they could cut the parts needed. I considered this for a few moments, then abandoned the idea entirely. Challenges were one thing, insanity was another.

In desperation I called Sara and described our plight. Yes, she responded, it was a common problem for anyone trying to renovate a house in the authentic country style. That was why so few people attempted to do what we were doing. It was simply too much bother chasing down century-old pieces and parts— not to mention the time required to restore old buildings compared to the relatively brief period it took to demolish them and build new ones. But, she continued almost mournfully, we had already chosen our path, so there was no turning back— unless, of course, we wanted to look at a more modern house that had just come on the market.

No, I said. No, thank you. We were quite content with our cottage and its slow but steady progress. It was just this niggling problem of the *cantarias*.

Sara sighed, then said she knew of a place where we might find them. There was a man, a *Senhor* Olímpio, who lived in a village not too far from ours. He was a contractor and sometimes collected stones from buildings that he demolished. He might have a few *cantarias* lying around, Sara said. But we should be very careful, she cautioned. He was not particularly scrupulous in his business dealings and was known to take advantage of foreigners whenever possible. And if we did seek him out, she added, we should tell him that Sara had sent us. He would treat us much better, and of course there might be something in it for her. She acknowledged that she was once again strapped for cash, and gave me crude directions to *Senhor* Olímpio's: go to Almoçageme, pass two bars, then left, pass another bar, then take a right, then ask the first person you see.

Barbara and I set off immediately to find the place, winding up the spine of the mountain, driving by fields of grass and grain. We passed a roadside market where Gypsy women sold vegetables, displaying them on bright scarves laid out on the ground. As we approached the village of Almoçageme, Barbara started counting the bars. It turned out to be easier than we had suspected. Since it was just after lunch, every little dive was belching out throngs of semi-inebriated patrons who swaggered off to return to work. Or, since it was a sunny day, they might be swaggering off to go fishing, which is where we suspected António had gone.

We found Olímpio's place down a dirt lane. It was surrounded by heaps of cast-off building materials and closely guarded by several skinny dogs, all suffering from various degrees of the mange. A man we assumed was Olímpio emerged from the modern house in the center of this menagerie, a very gruff expression on his face; it tempered substantially when he noticed the foreign license plates on our car. In fact, if greed ever had a smile, it went ear to ear on Olímpio. He immediately opened the car door on Barbara's side and helped her out, kissed her hand, and introduced himself, bowing at the waist. I stumbled out on the other side, thinking that the machinery of the cash register in Olímpio's mind was almost audible. I dodged two of the shaggiest dogs successfully before a third rubbed its slimy coat up against my leg. I made a mental note to burn the pants I was wearing.

Olímpio finally bounced around to acknowledge my presence, shaking my hand eagerly. He had a round, Cupid-like face with brilliant mischievous blue eyes.

"Well," he said, "you're here to buy some things, yes?"

Since we had never been approached in such a direct manner, I wasn't sure how to reply. I mumbled something about looking at what he might have, then comparing prices with other things we had seen.

"My prices are always right," Olímpio declared. "And you can pay in installments."

I felt I should introduce a note of caution. "Actually, we've heard that your prices are fairly high."

"Who told you that?" His eyes flashed, and I noticed one of the dogs urinating on our car bumper.

"Sara, actually. You know Sara? She sent us here."

"Her? Huh! She owes me money. That's why she says things like that. But you'll see. The merchandise will speak for itself. And if the price seems high, well then, that's because of the uniqueness of the piece. I have treasures here, things that you will not find anywhere else in the country. Look at this, for example."

He led us past a large pile of rubble. There, lying on the ground, visibly rusting away, was a pair of the largest forged iron doors I had ever seen. Olímpio kicked them.

"See these, madame?" He took Barbara's hand and pulled her close to the doors. "These are straight from one of the oldest villas in Sintra. Think how they will look at your house!"

I commented that they were very regal indeed but that our house was much more humble, a workman's cottage, and that what we had really come for was *cantarias*.

"Ah, *cantarias*! Of course." He paused to think for a moment, then snapped his fingers. "Yes, I've got them!"

Olímpio ran off behind the house and returned with a shovel. He paused briefly to kiss Barbara's hand again and to kick one of the dogs. Then, shovel in hand, he approached a large pile of debris and began to dig furiously.

Barbara looked at me expectantly. I shrugged. Two or three minutes went by, then suddenly Olímpio shrieked.

"Eh pa! Estão aqui!"

He motioned for us to approach, grinning broadly. Circumnavigating the mangy dogs, we went to the edge of the ditch Olímpio seemed to be excavating.

"Here," he said, tapping his shovel against something in the ditch. "*Cantarias.*"

I couldn't really see anything and said so. Olímpio seemed chagrined and, dropping to his knees, blew intensely on the ground. Enough dust lifted so that we could see what appeared to be several square centimeters of stone.

"You see now?" he asked. "And under this one there are more."

"*Cantarias?*" I asked.

"*Pois sim!*" he responded and returned to his frantic digging. A few minutes later he had succeeded in excavating a minor Acropolis. There were several stones, all very large, lying in a fragmented jumble. I was somewhat concerned because even without a tape measure I could see that, although squared off, they were several times larger than the window openings we needed to fill. I attempted to explain this to Olímpio and looked to Barbara for confirmation, only to find she had wandered off.

Olímpio was resolute in his response. "Listen. The size doesn't matter at all. These are the stones you want. You just tell the *pedreiros* to cut them to fit. These are very rare. You won't find them anywhere else."

That, I realized, was probably correct. And why had I expected to find them ready-made, tailored to the exact proportions required, as were all things in America? I kicked myself mentally. I hated such reminders of my Western mind-set. Somehow I had to overcome it, or I would never be able to fathom the ingrained Portuguese belief that whatever was available could be made to work.

"Take them all, one hundred fifty contos," Olímpio announced.

That was more than one thousand dollars and totally unreasonable. We only needed eight pieces—just enough to fill two window frames.

"*Não, obrigado.*"

My response prompted a minor tantrum from Olímpio. He made crude noises and banged on the stones with the shovel. "It's Sara's fault!" he cried. "Sending people here who are not inclined to buy. She does it because she owes me money.

She does it to tease me." He paused, and his mood changed dramatically. He had obviously reconsidered his approach. "Look," he began again, "you need the stones, yes?"

I replied that perhaps we needed the stones, but if they were that expensive, maybe we would just paint false *cantarias* on the facade of the house as our *pedreiro* had advised.

"You can't do that!" Olímpio seemed genuinely upset. "*Cantarias* are made to keep the evil spirits from entering the house. You must have them."

Evil spirits resided more likely in anything Olímpio had for sale here, I thought. "If that's the case," I replied, "with one hundred fifty contos we can hire several bodyguards."

"Look," Olímpio said. "I've already dug up the stones." He wiped his hand across his face, then showed it to me. "And I am sweating for you. You tell me how much the stones are worth."

I hadn't really expected this but decided to react as if I had been awaiting just such a moment. "Thirty contos and not an escudo more."

"Huh! My children! My dogs! Who is going to feed them? I can't do that." Then, in a very theatrical manner, Olímpio began shoveling the dirt back into the ditch, covering the stones. I knew it was my turn to say something, but I heard Barbara calling from beyond another heap of debris.

"Oh, the dogs!" I yelled.

With the same thought in mind, Olímpio and I both rushed over to where Barbara stood. But the dogs were nowhere in sight, and Barbara was pointing to a bit of porcelain sticking out from beneath a sheet of rotting plywood. "It's a claw-foot tub. It looks very nice."

Before we could say another word, Olímpio dove into the heap and pulled the tub into the daylight. It was a thing of grace and beauty with deftly sculpted legs and feet. And the very dainty, pale pink porcelain coating seemed to be intact.

I knocked on its side. "From a palace in Sintra, no doubt?"

Olímpio's eyes lit up. "This tub belonged to the queen

herself," he pronounced. "Look." He showed us an embossed shield just under the lip of the tub. "This is the emblem of the queen. This tub is worth a fortune! In fact, I don't think I want to sell it at all. I'm going to give it to a museum. Unless . . ." He took Barbara's hand again. "Unless Madame wants to bathe in the queen's tub. Then I can't say no."

I asked how much it would cost for "madame" to bathe in the tub.

Olímpio shifted from foot to foot. "Well," he said, "think what they will say back in Germany when you tell them you have the queen's bathtub."

I corrected him, telling him we were not Germans.

"Americans! Oh, then I can discount it even further. I have a cousin in Newark. Seventy-five contos only. And I deliver!"

The day was wearing on, and the scabby dogs had begun to circle us again, so I decided to try to speed up the negotiations. "Seventy-five contos for the lot," I said, holding out the money.

"*Sim,*" Barbara added, totally unaware of the topic under discussion.

Olímpio's face became a portrait of absolute despair. He took the money and just stared at it. "All right," he said. "Take it all and don't pay me. I don't care. I'll give it all to you in the interest of good relations. You'll come back to buy more, I know."

He made several gestures as if dispatching us mournfully. He kept the money, however, and we told him the location of the cottage.

"I'll deliver it all tomorrow," he called out after us as we walked toward the van. "But delivery is no longer included. See you then!"

We drove back to the cottage to find António, returned from his wanderings. He was drinking beer and sitting on top of a pile of *cantarias.*

Mason's Tools

16

WE DECIDED TO TAKE THE afternoon off after António had explained his lengthy absence. "I went to look for *cantarias*," he told us. It had been very arduous, he said, and as his explanation went on, I realized he must have motored over half of Portugal. Many false leads in many bars, António noted, and judging by his appearance, he must have been speaking the truth.

But the *cantarias* that António had discovered were very real—clean, square, and well cut, not like the amorphous rough stones we had just purchased and paid for at Olímpio's. And, António added, he had got them for free, or at least almost. We had to pay only for his time and the several rounds of drinks he was forced to buy to convince the owner of the stones to part with them for our noble cause.

We couldn't say no, of course. António was very sincere. I gave him the money, thinking to myself that he had figured out the perfect way to have a paid holiday.

António took the bills, rolled them up, and put them into his shirt pocket. He then announced that it was too late to start work that day, but there was plenty of time to visit the bar.

We declined his invitation and returned to Mummy's flat. Passing a butcher shop on the way, I stopped and got Barbara a special treat—two large and very appetizing tenderloins that the butcher swore were among the best cuts he had ever seen. Back at the flat, we crossed another day off the calendar—the continuing countdown to Mummy's arrival. Then, as Barbara went to change, I started to prepare the steaks. Since we had no broiler and no grill, the only way to cook the meat was in a pan. And to fit them into the pan available, I realized I would have to cut them. But when I attacked them with our sharpest knife, I quickly found I could barely make an impression. Somewhat chagrined, I gave the knife a good edge on the whetstone I carried for my tools and tried again. Same result. In fact, after another attempt, it became apparent that even though the two steaks had the look of quality beef, their true origin lay elsewhere. I tried a different angle, reasoning that perhaps I hadn't found the grain. But the reality was that there was no grain. The steaks were *cantarias* in disguise, back to taunt us.

Not wanting to give up without a fight, I remembered I had seen a meat grinder in one of the kitchen drawers. It was an old-style grinder with a thumbscrew that attached it to the counter. I installed it and prepared to make hamburger, feeding one of the sinewy steaks into its jaws. At first the grinder turned easily enough, although nothing came out through the blades. Then suddenly it locked and the handle turned no more. Still unwilling to admit defeat, I brought a chair over, mounted it, and with the added leverage of my weight, bore down on the grinder arm. Two little curls of ground meat emerged just before the grinder and I went flying across the room. I was left sitting on the floor, the grinder on my lap and the steak, for some odd reason, on the windowsill. Little research was required to discover what had happened. Glancing at the counter, I noticed that a huge chunk had disappeared—a piece now firmly locked in the grinder's thumbscrew. I made a mental note to buy some glue, a lot of glue. Mummy was coming soon, and it wouldn't do to have an injured countertop.

•

THE NEXT FEW DAYS WERE VERY AUSPICIOUS. THE SKY CLEARED, THE weather warmed, and spring arrived officially. Olímpio delivered the "queen's" bathtub but remained steadfast in his refusal to take back the *cantarias*. They were worth a lot of money, he said. We should try to sell them to another foreigner. We could make a fortune, he assured us. After Olímpio departed, António examined the stones. "All cracked," he said. "We can't use them."

I was upset. "But how could he sell us cracked stones?" I asked.

"This is Portugal," António responded. "Broken stones are the most expensive."

Paulo arrived that same day. He was a miniature version of António with lighter hair and a ruddy complexion. Fortunately, he would fit easily into spaces much too confined for António's bulk. Paulo was quicker, António stronger. And his presence seemed to improve António's mood so much that he actually came to work four days in a row. They were an effective team, saving countless matches as they passed cigarettes back and forth, lighting one from another, and chattering away in the local vernacular that I had to concentrate on to understand. Paulo was much more easygoing than António. He accepted all our bizarre suggestions as part of the job, pausing only occasionally to calmly explain why some of the more far-fetched ideas simply would not work here in Portugal.

We accomplished great things that first week after Paulo started work. Barbara worked her half-days steadily, fully in control now of the wheelbarrow. Materials that arrived on the main road made their way quickly down to the job site. She loaded up the wheelbarrow and adroitly guided it down the cobbled path, dodging the ever-present pack of dogs. But after every third trip she would go for a little coffee and expound on the difficulties of life with whoever might be in the bar. When her propensity for making hilarious blunders in Portuguese became known, her fame spread quickly, and people now came to the bar as soon as they found out she was there. They would then ply her with coffee and tongue twisters, sometimes even turning off the television, a great honor indeed.

Paulo was working steadily on Barbara's proposed arch in the living room. It was one of those things that António had guffawed at, saying the arch would be complicated and a waste of time. But when we presented the idea to Paulo, he said he would think about it. The next morning he arrived with a scale drawing. It became his pet project, and he embellished it even beyond what we had planned.

I was busy stripping the walls of their six-to-eight centimeters of lime plaster in the Portuguese fashion with hammer and chisel. But I was quickly growing bored with this tedious, time-consuming method. There had to be a better way, and I vowed that I would find it. Meanwhile, António had concurred that we needed a "cave"—a wine cellar—and had set about building one in the corner of the kitchen we had chosen. He was elaborating on the theme somewhat, spending extra time creating plaster moldings to frame the niche. But he seemed to be having so much fun doing it that we didn't question the extra expenditure. It would take only a few days, Paulo noted. We thought it would make a handsome addition and said no more, commenting on António's progress positively at the end of each day.

In the middle of all this good weather and hard work I suddenly realized that thirty days had gone by without the arrival of the water company. Since Paulo and I were quickly becoming good friends, I approached him and asked his opinion. He listened attentively, nodding, then asked who our *cunha* was. I wasn't familiar with the word. To accomplish anything in Portugal involving public services, Paulo said, you needed a *cunha*—someone who worked inside the utilities or someone with enough leverage to artfully or surreptitiously force your project through.

I told him we knew no one in the water company. He rolled his eyes and lit a cigarette. Then we couldn't possibly hope to accomplish anything, he said. The water company was notoriously corrupt, full of bureaucratic bimbos who could plot nothing but their next vacation or seminar in Italy. They spent most of their time fabricating excuses for doing nothing. They had no technical expertise. In short, they were the plague. If we really wanted water, Paulo declared, we should manufacture it ourselves.

When I told him the reasons a well wouldn't work in our location, Paulo agreed. But after a moment's thought he said that he had a distant cousin who worked at the water company. Although he wasn't in a position to actually do anything for us, he might be able to at least assess the situation and let us know how the village water project stood in reality—that is, beyond the words and promises of the water company managers.

I thought that would be fine but nevertheless decided to pay another visit to the municipal offices just to let them know that someone was watching and counting. So Barbara and I climbed into the van and set off for Sintra where we immediately discovered that new security measures had been put into effect at the water company. Rather than the open door through to the stairs that led to the executive offices, there was now a locked door with a buzzer. Only if someone, somewhere, pressed a button could we gain admission. We inquired and were informed that only people with appointments were allowed through now. "The executive offices were very busy," a woman at the information window told us. There were "great projects in the works," and the officials could not be disturbed at random. Just as she was making this declaration, we saw two waiters from a local café enter through the door laden with coffee, sweets, and *bagaço*. Obviously they weren't working too hard just now, I commented. The woman shrugged.

Not to be deterred, I insisted that we did have an appointment with the engineer Conception. No, I said, I didn't know why it was not in the ledger, but I had certainly made an appointment thirty days ago. I gave the woman my imaginary extended title, including what I thought was an appropriate number of doctoral degrees. She immediately perked up and went to a phone in the corner. After a lengthy discussion with someone, she finally buzzed us through.

Another hour and we were sitting in Conception's office watching her chain-smoke and file her nails while we waited for the village records to be delivered. When they finally appeared, Conception opened the folder and riffled through the pages with her nail file. I reminded her of what she had last told us—that a large holding tank would be installed on the hillside in thirty days, there would be water for everyone, and we would live happily ever after. Something had obviously gone wrong.

"Do you know," she said somewhat impatiently, "that there are trees on that hill?"

I replied that, yes, we knew. After all, we lived there, and the hill was part of the Sintra range, which is heavily forested everywhere.

"But there are a lot of trees," she said, "and no road!"

"Road?" I asked. "A road to where?"

She stared at me as if I were an idiot. "Why, a road to the spot where we want to put the tank, of course! How can we transport a huge tank up the hill without a road?"

I commented that I had been curious about that, too. A helicopter, perhaps? But I was convinced that the water company had a solution to the problem. Otherwise, why had it come up with this plan?

It was obvious that we were getting on Conception's nerves when she lit another cigarette, which meant she now had three going simultaneously. She pulled something out of the folder and spread it over her desk. "Do you see this?" she asked. "Do you know what this is?"

"Yes," I replied, acutely aware of the weight of all the titles I was brandishing about. "That's a topographical map."

"Correct," she said. "So show me the trees."

At first I thought it was a trick. "Topographical maps don't show trees," I finally said.

"Precisely! So how am I to know that there are trees on a hill when I make a plan?"

I casually suggested a visit to the site.

"I don't have time to visit every site," Conception declared. "I am in charge of this office. I just make the plans. It is up to others to do them. This is not my fault. No one told me about the trees."

I offered to cut the trees.

"And will you make the road, too?"

No, I admitted, I couldn't make the road. I hadn't been able to fit a bulldozer into my luggage when we came to Portugal, I said, trying to make a feeble joke.

She was not laughing, and I had the vague sensation that somehow, in some oblique manner, she relished the power she wielded over us and the village. A waiter arrived bringing her tea, and as he served her, I questioned the next step. Where did we go from here?

"Simple," she said. "Another plan will be made. I will order it today."

I inquired how long that would take.

"I don't know. It goes through another office. Probably sixty days."

"Sixty days!" I said.

"That's not very long," Conception said. "After all, the village has been without water for a thousand years."

There really wasn't much we could say in response to that, so we thanked her and left her office. I stopped at the information window and asked who was responsible for making project plans. There were several people involved, and we made appointments with all of them, then made another appointment with Conception for the same day. We were determined to keep them on their toes.

Countryside

17 THE NEXT DAY AT THE SITE,
we arrived to find a strange man circling the house taking mea-
surements. He was short and wiry and wore a checkered beret.
António introduced him as Alberto, a very rare bird in Portugal
because, he said, Alberto was both an electrician and a plumber.
Hard enough to find one or the other, António declared, but a
man who knows both trades, this was something extraordinary!

And he was willing to work for very little money—so little, in fact, that we would hardly know he was there.

I reminded António that I intended to do the wiring and the plumbing myself.

"Who is going to make the cement then?" he asked. "If you're busy doing that, who is going to run the mixer?"

Actually I had intended, in a strange American fashion, to do both. But I saw António's logic. In a few weeks the cement mixer would have to be run almost continuously. And that would be at the same time the plumbing and electrical systems had to be installed. Fair enough, but yet another hard rap on the budget.

"And you want to be in by July?" António said, pressing his point. "But if you don't want him here, I will send him away. Oh, Alberto!"

I asked António cautiously how much we had to pay him.

"Cheap," António replied. "You pay him the same as you pay us, three thousand a day. Electricians and plumbers always get more, but since you're a friend, Alberto will work for the minimum."

I gave in and told Barbara what I had done.

"He has a very nice face," she said. "Kind of Goya-like. Maybe he can model for me later."

So Alberto joined the crew. I spent several minutes talking to him and discovered that he knew very little about either plumbing or electricity, but he was pleasant enough and had a great sense of humor. He was also a cousin of António's and Paulo's, and for no particular reason at all, it somehow felt good that the renovation would be a family effort.

After explaining to Alberto the fundamentals of the plan, Paulo pulled me aside. He had spoken with his cousin in the water company—Garganta Profunda—"Deep Throat," we had agreed to call him since Paulo had seen the same movie. Things did not look good for the village, it seemed. Since there were only a few hundred people involved, it was a very insignificant project. Therefore, they had suspended further action indefinitely.

"But we were there just yesterday," I said. "Conception told us they were making new plans."

"She lied," Paulo said. "She just told you that to appease you. Believe me, nothing is happening."

But Paulo's cousin had a suggestion. We should write a petition, have everyone in the village sign it, then present it to the municipality. In that way the municipality might be able to exert some pressure on the water company and coerce it to do something.

It was certainly worth a try, I thought. I thanked Paulo and returned to Mummy's flat to pick up my cheap Portuguese typewriter. On the way back to the village I stopped to buy some *papel selado,* the official paper, and some fiscal stamps of various denominations. Returning to the cottage, I picked a corner I thought safe from dust and began to peck away. But I was only a few sentences into the document when I realized I had absolutely no grasp whatsoever of Portuguese legalese—or, rather, what I assumed to be legalese, that universal and obscure language intelligible only to lawyers and bureaucrats. I asked Paulo for some help and within minutes he, António, and Alberto were involved in a tremendous argument over the choice of opening words. I called a truce and announced that I was going to *Senhor* Pimenta for assistance. He should know what we were doing anyway since he was the spokesman for the village.

Senhor Pimenta slowly emerged from the small doorway that led to the counter in his store and assumed his position behind the ancient olive jar and the brass weights and scale. He thought a petition was an excellent idea but suggested that we get a lawyer to draw up the document. When I told him it was my belief that no matter how bad the water company might be, lawyers were worse, he nodded in agreement, and we shared a brief moment of universal sentiment.

Senhor Pimenta said he would help me write the document as long as he was not the first to sign. If his signature came first, he said, people might assume he was responsible for the words in the document, and, well, people took the written word very seriously. I said that would be no problem, and together we managed to create a fair specimen of literary Portuguese. I typed up a final copy, put a number of stamps on it to make it look official, then took the final product back to the cottage for the *pedreiros'* inspection. They had several comments, but in the end they pronounced it serviceable. They also suggested that we leave the petition in the bar since everyone passed through at some point during the day or night. And this was a perfect excuse to stop work immediately and head down there.

At the bar we presented the petition to José, who examined it carefully. It would never do, he said. He had an uncle who was a lawyer so he knew quite a bit about legal documents, and the third sentence was not appropriate. We could not "demand" water, he said. We must "request" water. The wording just wouldn't do.

While António was downing his third vermouth, I told José that we had already "requested" water several times to no avail. Obviously it was a time for stronger words.

No, no, José said. If we wanted the petition to stay in the bar, we must change the words.

Rather than argue, I got the typewriter and, in the middle of a gathering crowd, changed the offending words. I put the document back on the bar. José scanned it briefly and nodded his approval. Now, he asked, who is going to be the first to sign?

I said I would sign first, but he held up his hand. That would never do. A Portuguese should be the first to sign, he said. No offense intended, but the water company might not think much of a document signed at the top by a foreigner. No, someone else must sign first.

I turned the petition around to face him as he handed Alberto another vermouth. But José shook his head. No, he said, he couldn't be the first to sign, either. It wouldn't be good for him because he had no commercial license for the bar, and the water company could cause problems for him.

I addressed the other patrons in the bar, holding the petition up in the air. Who will sign first, I asked in a loud voice. But I noticed everyone was either staring at the ground or at the television, which for some reason was not turned on. Come on, I said, someone must want to go first. There was a long silence. Then, after another moment, António slammed his glass down on the bar. All right, he said. He would sign it first if someone bought him a drink. José replied that he would gladly buy António a drink but that he really should not sign at all since he was not a resident of the village.

Huh, António snorted. Not a resident? He had been born in the village! Even though it wasn't intended to happen that way, nevertheless it had. Besides, he still had seventeen relatives residing here which gave him plenty of authority. He asked if anyone had any further objections. No one did, of course, so António directed José to bring him his drink and the petition.

With great ceremony and relish António swirled his drink then gulped it down. After staring at the petition for a moment, he asked for a pen. No one moved. José shrugged. He had only a pencil, he said, and it wouldn't do to sign in pencil. This was an official document and must be signed in pen, a pen with blue ink. Everyone murmured in agreement. I said I would get one, but António was up before I could reach the door. He would get the pen. It was his duty if he was going to be the first to sign. He would be right back, he said, as he climbed on his motorcycle and rode away. That was Tuesday afternoon. He did not return until Friday.

Local Transport

18

WE HAD COME TO REGARD
Sandra's soirées as a welcome interlude in our more serious
venture of renovating the cottage. Her parties were also the
ideal escape from reality. We quickly lost track of the various
diplomats, royals, and other gentry that we met seated at the
dinner table. But the fact that these people were so intangible
lent an air of surrealism to the entire event. At one point we

had even formulated a theory that they were not who they said they were at all. They were actors hired by Sandra and cast in different roles purely to entertain us. But this theory failed to hold water when, once again, flesh to flesh with them, it was very evident that they were the real thing. No one could wear jewelry and expensive perfume so well except those accustomed to doing it often.

I once asked Sandra what Barbara and I were doing among all this splendor. "Well," she had answered, "you're Bob's friends, and you seem to appreciate the food and wine more than the others who eat and drink like this all the time. You can talk to anyone in almost any language, and—don't tell Barbara—the women think you have a great tush."

On this particular evening Barbara and I took our Riedel wineglasses and retreated to a corner. It was the perfect location from which to observe the arrival of the "glitterati" and a good place for me to hide my "tush," of which I was now painfully aware. The guests meandered in, fashionably late, as was the local custom. At some of Sandra's parties the last guests arrived only as the first guests departed—a tag team sort of event.

Now we watched as they came in from the evening chill, kissed Sandra in a variety of ways depending on their degree of intimacy, then deposited their collection of haute couture overcoats on a long couch appointed for that purpose. As always Barbara and I were dazzled by their perfect teeth, the one thing they all had in common. But suddenly, as we drank our wine and rated smiles on a musical scale, a very unusual man entered. Although he was dressed as impeccably as everyone else, the item that set him apart was a highly polished band of stainless steel that covered his eyes and wrapped around his head. It was very unconventional under any circumstances, but it was the casual elegance of the object that immediately drew our attention. A sudden hush fell over the room as others also noticed the young man's appearance.

Sandra, ever the perfect hostess, took advantage of the silence to announce his name. "This is Hugues, everyone. Hugues, let me take you around and introduce you." One by one, she presented him to her other guests. Hugues would shake the men's hands and kiss the women on the cheek. Then he would lift his left hand slowly and let it wander over the face of whomever he had just been introduced to.

It was clear, even with the band of steel around his head, that Hugues was an extraordinarily attractive man. His face was lean and tan, perfectly proportioned. His sandy blond hair was swept back smoothly under the sheath of steel. When he finally made his way to our corner, I greeted him in French, the language he had used with the other guests. To my surprise he answered me in English.

"Your French is almost perfect, with only a soupçon of an American accent," he said. "Congratulations."

Hugues tilted his head and seemed to sniff the air. "And you, madame," he said to Barbara, "you are American also?"

"Yes," Barbara replied.

"It is easy to tell by your scent," Hugues said. "Since I have been blinded, I am forced to use other senses, and your perfume, although Jolie Madame by Balmain, is not the one made in France. You are wearing the American version, *n'est-ce pas?*"

"Yes, I am," Barbara stammered.

"Do not be nervous. It is not a reason to be chagrined. And what are you doing in Portugal?"

The question was obviously directed at Barbara, and she tried to answer as Hugues raised his hand and began to run his fingers over her face.

"We are renovating a house."

"I see," he said, caressing her chin. "Your face is very well proportioned. I am sure the rest of your body is the same. Renovating a house in Portugal? I have heard nothing but horror stories. You should write a book about it if you ever finish the thing."

Sandra led Hugues off to talk with her other guests while Barbara and I tried to regain our composure. It was only later that we learned the complete story about Hugues. It seems he was a writer living in New York, and one night his apartment was broken into by a thief. Hugues discovered the theft in progress and during the scuffle that followed the thief threw a flask of acid he was carrying into Hugues's face. Plastic surgery had repaired the skin, but medicine could do nothing for his eyes. Hugues had just finished a book about the experience called *La Lumière Assassiné*—*The Assassinated Light*.

Needless to say, Hugues was the center of attention that evening. He was a wonderful storyteller in several languages and had trained his remaining senses to such a degree that they were able to compensate for his lack of vision. The women present were more than intrigued. At one point several of them vied for the privilege of accompanying him out to the back garden so he could relieve himself.

These parties were great fun. What a wonderful life we could have, we thought, if we could finish the damned house and spend every night here at Sandra's. But we had the energy to attend only once or twice a month. We found that if we stayed out late, it dulled us for the following morning of work. And there were only a few weeks left before Mummy would arrive to reclaim her apartment.

Cascais Fishermen

19

ONE OR TWO DAYS AFTER
Sandra's latest party, I was summoned to the Serviço dos Estrangeiros, the Bureau for Foreign Residents, in Cascais. It was
several months since we had last heard from them, and we were
beginning to worry that our file, and hence our lives, had been
somehow misplaced. Everyone warned us that they were noto-
rious bureaucrats and we should not expect to hear from them

for years. But unfortunately we had to rely on their paperwork considerably. All in all, it was a totally confusing mess.

We wanted to buy a house, and to do so we were required to import foreign funds because we were not legal residents. We had to apply to the Bank of Portugal for permission to import these funds. And the Bank of Portugal—which really wasn't a bank at all but rather another collection of bureaucrats stuffed away in an office somewhere—wanted to know the reason for the purchase of the house because that dictated, more or less, how it treated our request. Since we intended to live in the house, we indicated that it was for residence. But in order to reside there—or, rather, in order for the Bank of Portugal to think that we were going to reside there—we had to apply for residency. Once we had applied for residency, we sent a copy of the application to the Bank of Portugal bureaucrats, which mollified them temporarily. They issued a bulletin "condoning" the import of our foreign funds within thirty days. But within that thirty days—which, by the way, began to run the moment the bulletin was signed and not the day it was delivered to us two weeks later—we somehow had to import the money, establish a time for the "closing" on the sale of the house, then actually go to the closing. That, of course, had proved to be impossible. So, as everyone was forced to do, we had to constantly "float" the importation bulletin back to the Bank of Portugal to request an extension, continuing to hope that somehow, someday, everything would finally coalesce into a sale.

Now, in addition to those labyrinthine official procedures, there was the residency question. A hefty tax called SISA had to be paid unless the house was to be used strictly for the owner's occupancy. To establish that, one naturally had to be a resident; otherwise, how could one reside in the house legally? But buying a house alone did not ensure obtaining residency. Nothing that simple. To obtain residency you had to prove several things: first, that you had a reason to reside in Portugal. And according to the people at the Serviço dos Estrangeiros, there was no valid reason to reside here. If you cited beauty or climate, they would counter with the description of an idyllic temperate area in your home country. If you somehow convinced them you had a reason to reside here, you were asked your profession. We had pondered this for months, aware that our response would weigh heavily on our application. Foreigners who arrived to take jobs from Portuguese were not looked upon kindly. So in the end we told a half-truth. I was a writer and Barbara an artist.

Next, we had to have proof of sustenance, and here the road became rather rocky. The people at the Bureau for Foreign Residents would not accept our currency importation license as proof of anything. In fact, they seemed to scorn the Bank of Portugal entirely. They also would not accept bank statements from abroad. What was required was evidence of means of support with funds already in Portugal or proof of a means of continuing income from abroad. We had neither. We had some money wired to our local bank in order to appease them—not much but at least enough to cover our sustenance for several months. When we proudly showed this to them, they replied that it was not sufficient. Since we were feeling bold that day, we inquired exactly how much would be sufficient. They wouldn't tell us directly. Instead they meandered into discussions of inflation and interest, then began to argue among themselves. It was no use questioning them further. They seemed to be adamant about their noncommittal. We merely continued submitting our documents and hoped for the best.

But we always enjoyed going to Cascais. The coastal road led around the fringe of the Sintra mountains and offered rugged views of granite cliffs as they plunged suddenly down to the sea. A few hearty villages were scattered along the road, perched on the crests of narrow green valleys planted with lemon orchards. And there was usually a strong salty breeze blowing up from the extensive stretch of sandy beaches that lined the last few kilometers to town.

Cascais itself was a paradox. Advertised in tourist

brochures as a "quaint fishing village," this disguise was quickly wearing thin. Although craggy-faced fishermen still assembled each morning by their nets and colorful, albeit shoddy boats, they no longer put out to sea in search of a catch. Instead, they had become picturesque ornaments to a burgeoning cosmopolitan population. Cascais, with its large pleasure harbor and enticing beaches, was slowly becoming the Portuguese mecca for the very type of people who attended Sandra's parties. The European elite seemed to enjoy the variety of amenities the village provided, and so they had adopted it as their new playground.

In addition to the beachside villas these people had built, a grand array of international eateries had sprung up. One could wander from an "authentic" English pub to a wood-fired pizzeria, stopping at a German *Biergarten* in between. Add to this the variety of golf courses, health spas, and exclusive nightclubs, and all the prerequisites of society's upper crust were satisfied. So they came to eat, drink, and play in the sun or else at the casino in nearby Estoril. And in their wake, during the summer, came tourists who paused just long enough to take pictures of the barefoot fishermen clad in their long woven caps. The fishermen seemed to enjoy it and readily admitted that the waters around Cascais had become too polluted to support marine life anyway—no doubt due to the diligence of our friends at the Municipal Services.

Today at the Foreign Office in Cascais, an elegant but seedy old building with crumbling yellow plaster, stuccoed rosettes, and bare wires hanging from the walls, I stood in line holding copies of all the papers we had submitted. It seemed to be a very emotional affair for the others gathered there, I noticed, and quite often tempers flared and people broke into tears. A large percentage of the "petitioners" did not speak Portuguese and were dealt with in a very brusque manner. Fortunately, speaking Portuguese, I had been able to make friends with the two women who ran the counter. Although I was unaware to what extent they might be helpful, I thought it best to seek out allies wherever and whenever possible. The only problem was that one of them looked exactly like engineer Conception. In fact, even their nail files were identical. But with extreme emotional control I managed to put the resemblance aside and proceed with exaggerated courtesy.

The two women recognized me that day and told me it would be just a minute. Forty-five minutes later they came out and ushered me through the throngs of crying women and screaming children into a dark, somber office I had never seen before. There were four desks around the perimeters of the room occupied by pious-looking men in dark suits who hunched over piles of yellowing paper. Bare lightbulbs hung from the ceiling in the center of the room, a radio was playing somewhere, and clouds of smoke hovered in the air. It was in an office just like this one that Franz Kafka had worked and obtained his inspiration. Of that I had no doubt.

The two women directed me to a chair, then left me to my fate. No one took notice of me for several minutes, then suddenly, as if on cue, all four of the men rose from their chairs and approached. How did they coordinate that so well? I didn't have time to ask, but they had obviously come to question me.

"Why do you want to live in Portugal?" one of the men asked.

I had anticipated that and had contrived a new answer. "Because," I said, "my father was Portuguese, and I want to know the country of his provenance."

They were silent for a moment, regarding each other with a variety of facial expressions. Had I stumped them? Had I finally come up with a logical, acceptable answer? Apparently not, because one of the men took the lead and began clucking with his tongue and shaking his head. "If your father was Portuguese, you are at the wrong office," he said. I should be at the emigrant's office because people of Portuguese ancestry fell under its jurisdiction.

I was also prepared for that and told them the truth. My

father had died when I was thirteen, and I had discovered my Portuguese heritage only a few years ago—too late to ascertain my father's lineage or the whereabouts of his extended family. I knew only that they came from the Azores Islands.

The four men regarded one another and then began a protracted discussion about the beauty and climate of the Azores. None, it appeared, had ever been there. Their conversation ended abruptly, and they bore down on me again.

"What is your profession?"

Again I knew it would not do to tell them that I built a house occasionally. Portugal was full of itinerant contractors, most of them unscrupulous. "I'm a writer," I said without blinking an eye.

They didn't seem to be listening. Something somewhere else had caught their attention. I listened and heard nothing but the droning of the radio in the background. Then, after a few minutes, inexplicably, all four men expressed their condolences to me, shook my hand, and one of them led me out of the office, saying that they would be in touch.

I wandered down the cobblestoned lanes of Cascais dumbfounded. Certainly I had not been subjected to the intense grilling I had expected. What exactly had happened? I found out a few days later that the Challenger Space Shuttle had exploded during my interrogation. The four men had heard about it on the radio, and the sudden curtailment of my interview was their way of expressing compassion and commiseration.

Two weeks later I received my formal residency papers in the mail.

The Chapel

20
AFTER SOME PROCRASTINA-
tion, the water company petition was finally signed by all the
villagers. It was an arduous task, convincing them to put their
names on a piece of paper. Some preferred not to sign because
they already had water service of some sort—be it from a shallow well or from an ancient spring. They thought that signing a
petition would somehow compromise their honor and the pres-

tige of having already accomplished what others could not. I spent countless hours talking about the general needs of the village as a whole and extolling the virtues of democracy and the equality of all men.

For others it was merely a matter of fear. They didn't want any document with their name on it to fall into the government's hands. They remembered the pre-1974 era too well and were sure someone would come knocking on their door in the middle of the night to chastise them for their political activity. But after several drinks and gentle persuasion, they, too, came around, finally convinced that a water main entering their house was not an invasion of their privacy or a way for the government to spy on them.

Once the signatures had been collected, Barbara and I set off for Sintra. We shared a marvelous sense of accomplishment. We had done a great service for the village—for mankind, even. We wanted to see the look on Conception's face when we presented her with this legal document. We wanted to see her cringe and perhaps even impale herself on her nail file. Or, if not that, then at least feel a modicum of guilt for forestalling the water project in the last village lacking municipal water in the entire Sintra area.

But our imagined victory was short and sparkless. Yet another new security system had been installed, and it was almost impossible to pass through the public area directly into the executive offices. Besides the electric door buzzer, a guarded gate had been added. I imagined briefly that all this had been done for our benefit—top-rank security to keep crazy foreigners from reaching the inner sanctum of the corrupt and thereby forcing them to at least appear to be hard at work.

Not to be intimidated, we stepped up to the information window and announced our intention of delivering an official document to Conception. When asked what it was, I told the woman attending me, who rolled her eyes, pulled out a fat ledger labeled "Petitions," and opened it to the very last page.

Feeling suddenly much smaller, we handed her the petition and watched as she scanned it, then said it was not proper because it lacked a 50-escudo stamp. Since I had learned never to travel anywhere without these stamps, I still had a number of them left over from other frustrating endeavors, so I pulled the proper stamp from my wallet, licked it, and slapped it on the petition. The woman frowned and gave the document a violent smash with a huge inked rubber stamp. She numbered it, made a note in the ledger, and asked me if there was anything else.

"What happens next?" I inquired.

"O senhor aguarde a resposta."

We should wait for an answer. Of course. And if it didn't come in this lifetime, well, swing by in the next one and see if your number has come up yet.

Since that was not one of our favorite responses, we decided to wait just thirty days. I respectfully postponed the appointments I had already scheduled with Conception and others, citing my required attendance at "hydraulic seminars" in Rome and Vienna. When I returned, I told the woman, I would share any knowledge gleaned from these meetings with the water company staff.

She seemed totally unimpressed and scribbled something illegible in the appointment book. We thanked her, elbowed our way through the crowd, and left the building.

•

A FEW DAYS LATER BA ARRIVED ON THE JOB SITE. SINCE HE WAS renowned throughout the Sintra area as the best *servente* in Portugal, we were very lucky indeed to have him. António had hinted several times that he was a personal friend of Ba's and might be able to persuade him to come and work for us. We must be careful, though, António warned. Ba had never worked for foreigners before, and I should continue the story about my family having come from the Azores. Otherwise Ba might become afraid and disappear.

I knew as soon as I arrived early that morning that something was different. The path to the gate was cleared of debris and neatly raked. The mounting piles of rubble had somehow been sculpted and now assumed a tidy shape. And most amazing of all, mortar had already been mixed and awaited the arrival of the first *pedreiro*. Suddenly what I had considered a battleground began to look like a proper project, organized and professional. Adding Ba to the team would make a great difference. I could finally work on the doors and windows. Maybe we could even finish on schedule!

I found Ba in the cottage, just finishing the sweeping of the floor. It had never been so clean. I introduced myself and thanked him for what he had done so far. He averted his eyes and mumbled that it was all part of the job. He returned to sweeping with incredible vigor.

I was a little shocked. I had expected a *servente,* a tender, to be much younger. Ba must have been at least sixty, short, thin, and exceptionally wiry. He had tight, kinky red hair and wore a T-shirt that said ESPRIT.

When Paulo, Alberto, and even António arrived, they all entered the cottage, looked around, and noted the tidiness. *"É o melhor,"* they said, pointing at Ba.

He was the best. I nodded in agreement. Ba seemed not to listen and continued sweeping.

"And he's very strong," António said, pumping his arm up and down.

I took the cue. "Can he lift the cement mixer?" I asked.

António laughed. "No, only I can do that. But he can do other things. Watch."

António shouted something to Ba who immediately put down his broom and fell to the floor. He lay still, facedown, for an instant, then slowly raised his entire body off the floor with one hand. Next, he somehow managed to lift his body so that he was doing a one-hand handstand—all this while smoking a cigarette. It was very impressive. Finished with his act, Ba let himself down, picked up his broom, and went back to sweeping.

"And there's more good news," António announced. He

had found someone to take away the mounting piles of debris. This was good news indeed. The very mass of the piles had begun to concern us, and it seemed there was now more debris than house. The huge mounds had begun to obstruct the path in front of the cottage, and the neighbor across the way had already complained that dust was blowing into her house.

"And you don't have to pay," António said. It seemed a friend of Alberto's, an aspiring bullfighter, was constructing a ring for himself and needed fill. He would be here within an hour, and the problem would be solved.

We began to work in earnest, and everything seemed right with the world. Even Barbara showed up early, saying that she was on a new schedule. It was about an hour later when Alberto came up to me. "We have a problem," he said.

He led me downstairs and over into a corner of what would someday, perhaps even in this decade, be our kitchen. We had piled some of the debris we had found in the house there— suitcases, old wine flasks, a number of bizarre metal objects and the two old steamer trunks.

Alberto put his finger to his lips to indicate silence, then gestured toward one of the dilapidated trunks. I leaned over and looked inside. There, in a corner, tightly curled up among shredded newspaper, was a mother cat and her six newborn kittens.

"I heard some noise," Alberto said.

I went out and called Barbara. She came down completely covered in red dust, complaining that António was making her hold flooring tiles while he trimmed them with a huge masonry saw.

We showed her our discovery, and she was immediately enthralled. "We have to get food and water for the mother," she said. "Can we keep them all?"

I shook my head. "Where? We promised Mummy we wouldn't have any pets."

"How about here?"

But the house had no windows or doors, I said—not even

a place we could put them for a few days without having to move them. It really wasn't appropriate at all.

As I spoke, António appeared, obviously alerted, and went over to the trunk. He started cooing in a high voice I wouldn't have thought him capable of, then reached down into the trunk to stroke the kittens. A moment later he screamed and jumped away from the trunk. Our first thought was that the mother cat had scratched him, but no, it was something other than that. António was jumping up and down and slapping at his legs and sides.

"*Pulgas!*" he yelled.

Then we knew. Fleas! Paulo, who had just started to enter the room until he heard António's pronouncement, immediately fled. Alberto stopped laughing and streaked out to the garden. I suddenly began to feel itchy, too, as did Barbara. We didn't want to miss the spectacle of mammoth António jumping up and down, ripping at his clothes, but when we felt the first bites, we, too, ran into the garden and began scratching frantically. Alberto and Paulo, laughing hysterically, gave us a wide berth.

Later, after we had managed to disinfest ourselves, the cat, the kittens, and the ground floor of the cottage, we realized that the event was an omen. Almost every house in Portugal had a name, and we had been looking for an appropriate one for the cottage. Someone had neglected to name it previously, probably due to the split between the two sisters. And since we would be living in the house someday, it had to have some sort of identification. There were no numbers in the countryside to aid postmen. They worked strictly by house names.

It was Barbara who mentioned it first. "House of the Little Cats," she said. "Why not?"

We discussed it very briefly, and House of the Little Cats it became—Casa dos Gatinhos. As always we had included the workers in our discussion. Alberto laughed loudly, Paulo nodded approval, and António confirmed our choice. All the other houses in the village had the names of animals or flowers, he said. Therefore, it was appropriate. António went even further. Since it was an important moment in the history of the house, it was only fitting that we go to the bar and announce our selection. "That way," he said, "everyone will know the name by tonight."

I couldn't resist a jab at António. "We had considered calling it the House of Fleas."

António replied with his usual coarse invective as we all walked and scratched our way down to the bar.

•

SEVERAL HOURS LATER WE HEARD THE TRUCK ARRIVE. EMERGING TO greet this temporal savior who would relieve us of tons of accumulated dust and debris, I immediately saw a problem—the truck was immense. When António mentioned that someone was coming, I had envisioned a small four-wheel-drive vehicle able to maneuver down the cobblestones and the narrow path between the chapel and adjacent structures. But this was a huge dump truck. As it was, I couldn't figure out how he had gotten as far as he had, and in reverse.

And I had only to sniff the air to realize that the driver must have had an extended lunch that included at least several *bagaços*. He stumbled out of the cab and greeted us, then began a prolonged conversation about bullfighting with Alberto.

I pulled Paulo aside and asked him what we were going to do.

He seemed surprised. "About what?"

"The driver's drunk."

"Of course he is," Paulo said. "It's after lunch. It's the custom."

"But," I persisted, "how is he going to get the truck out of here? Once it's loaded, he'll never make it back up the hill."

Paulo put his arm around my shoulder. Didn't we want the rubble removed? Well then, I should relax. This was Portugal, not America. Everyone knew that things were different here, but they always had a way of working out. Just like with the name of the house, right? I said I would try to relax, but I made a mental note to hide as far away as possible when the truck was ready to leave.

We borrowed a few shovels and went to work filling up the cavernous bed of the truck. The driver and Alberto went off to the bar to "discuss business." I shuddered and shoveled and tried to think pleasant thoughts. Nevertheless, the nightmare of being responsible for demolishing half the village remained in my mind. I kept having visions of the truck plunging down the cobblestoned alley. How much damage could it possibly do? Would the first few houses absorb the impact, or would the truck go right through them and continue down into the valley? I felt as if I was making a bomb. Each shovelful of rubble was another ounce of TNT. Maybe we should call the whole thing off. Who was responsible for all this anyway? We didn't even own the house yet. Maybe after the truck had destroyed the village, we could simply say that we were just guest workers from another country and sneak away into the forest.

An hour later we had the truck filled to overflowing. I had warned António that we should stop halfway, but he had insisted on filling it to the maximum and then some. He went down to fetch Alberto and the driver, and the three of them returned an hour later.

I took one look at the driver and was eternally grateful that he was driving the truck. He was certainly in no shape to walk. He had one arm around Alberto and the other around António, his feet dragging along the dirt path. This was just perfect, I thought. It obviously explained how the most bizarre accidents occurred here, how cars ended up in treetops. No one accepted driving as a responsibility. It was more like a contact sport. Finish driving school and hit the road running. We had visited a driving school once. There were lots of charts and endless classes explaining the mysteries of the internal combustion engine, but very little time was actually spent on the road. Ten minutes, perhaps. Or if you were really in a hurry, you bribed the instructor and skipped the road lessons completely.

Our truck driver took one look at his load, spit on his hands, and rubbed them together gleefully, then climbed in behind the wheel. I immediately took off down the dirt path, not wanting to be a witness in the court proceedings that were sure to follow. I heard the engine start and rev up, then the sound of hard rubber burning on the cobblestones. The group of *pedreiros* cheered the driver on in loud voices, and after a cacophony of squeals, yelps, and squeaks came silence. It seemed that he had made it up the alley after all. I could relax.

Turning back I saw António, Alberto, Paulo, Ba, and Barbara staring up the lane. And as I rounded the corner past the cottage, I, too, could see the predicament. The truck had not quite made it to the top. It was perched at a full stop just on the brink of the upper road. Or, rather, it appeared to be at a full stop. Looking more closely, I could see that even with the wheels locked, the truck was beginning to slide slowly back down the hill. Armageddon was definitely at hand.

António shouted something, and everyone scattered. Villagers appeared at their windows. The woozy truck driver, finally aware that something was wrong, gunned his motor and set his wheels in motion, but they had little effect beyond pouring clouds of black smoke into the air.

Like everyone else, I hid, clambering behind the cottage's garden wall. I waited there for the inevitable crash that seemed hours in coming. When it did come, it was even louder than I had thought possible, and it was accompanied by a huge cloud of smoke. Peeping over the wall, I briefly admired the vibrant colors of the billowing column of dust as it rose in the air. It was not often that circumstances combined to give one the opportunity to witness the awesome beauty of total destruction.

A few minutes later I ventured around the corner. Much to my relief the truck had not destroyed half of the countryside, but it had demolished a good section of the rear of the village chapel. Through the gaping hole in the wall I could see various Catholic paraphernalia strewn about the rubble. There were pews and an altar. The truck driver, running his hands over Jesus on the crucifix, announced that he was unharmed.

Most of the village had gathered by now, and I thought there must have been a similar scene when the water company had first arrived. Were they going to throw stones at us? Finally, *Senhor* Pimenta appeared to pronounce sentence. He looked at the damaged chapel and at the teetering truck that protruded from its side. Who was responsible? he asked.

I shuffled my feet and hummed a silly little tune. I fooled no one. The drunken truck driver was pointing at me!

I proclaimed my innocence. I hadn't asked the driver to come or condoned his bringing the truck down the cobble-stoned alley. Nor was I responsible for the fact that he was more than slightly drunk.

Senhor Pimenta heard me out. "All right," he said finally. "If the man is drunk, who paid for his drinks?"

An honorable solution, I thought. José the bartender. Let him who causes inebriation pay for its consequences.

I was somewhat more than chagrined when José also pointed at me.

"What!" I said. "I wasn't even at the bar!" But I soon realized what must have happened. José had put the driver's drinks on our tab!

"Tinha que ser," António said. "It had to be." He thought the least we could do was buy the poor fellow a few drinks. After all, he wasn't asking to be paid for his services, and the truck was a very expensive dump model and . . .

Senhor Pimenta held up his hand. "You bought the drinks, so you will have to fix the chapel," he said to Barbara and me. "But," he said with a wink, "you don't have to go to confession and no Ave Marias."

And so we spent the next three days fixing the chapel walls after a tow truck had come to extricate the monstrous dump truck. And, I noticed unhappily, the pile of rubble left from the chapel repairs was almost as big as the one the dump truck had finally carted away.

The Fireplace

21

A FEW DAYS LATER MUMMY showed up for an inspection of her apartment. Although she arrived under the guise of removing some of her personal belongings from storage, it was obvious that she meant to case the flat to see if we were perverts and miscreants, as most tenants were assumed to be. She was a gracious, nervous, elderly woman who spoke baronial English and had just the right amount of gray hair. She inquired kindly about how our project was going and if we were enjoying the area. She squinted at Barbara's pictures and asked if that was really what she wanted to paint. Then she gathered up a few small items from a locked room in the apartment and feigned departure. And oh, yes, would we be out by July 1 as agreed?

Barbara and I stared at each other, each of us hoping the other would be the first to commit perjury. I finally said yes, of course, no problem. Although I was sure the tenor of my voice gave us away, Mummy seemed satisfied with the answer. She probably thought we were dependable because we were Americans. Little did she realize the subtle effect that Portuguese civilization was having on us.

The next day I arrived early at the site, even before Ba had appeared. It was an important day because I was planning to build the smoke shelf and throat of the Rumsford fireplace I had been constructing in the living room. Although the Rumsford theory of fireplace construction had been brought from Europe to America by Benjamin Franklin, this was, as far as I knew, the first to be built on the Iberian peninsula. Portuguese fireplaces were much like their American tract-built counterparts—too deep and geometrically askew to actually produce any heat. They were cosmetic, for viewing only. Rumsford fireplaces, on the other hand, were for heating. They had shallow fireboxes with elegant tapered firebacks and narrow throats to squeeze maximum heat out of combustibles.

I faced two problems constructing a Rumsford here. First, for some odd reason the laws of physics did not apply in Portugal. We had seen water run uphill in the village—that was, when water ran at all. We had seen hot air sink instead of rise. We had seen engineer Conception's file in constant motion, without removing an ounce of fingernail. It was a country full of natural wonders, and we never doubted for a moment that the Virgin had appeared in Fatima. It made perfect sense in view of the other miraculous phenomena we had seen.

What was the reason for this? I speculated long and hard and came to the conclusion that Mother Nature had simply given in, as we had, to the ineffable Portuguese logic. Certainly she had tried to exert herself but in the end had found the indigenous psyche too intractable and perverse. Natural laws had simply suspended themselves until further notice, when some sort of order was imposed on the prevailing chaos. With all this in mind, I was trying to be extra careful with my calculations. If a certain size chimney tile was required, I automatically went a size larger. And I intended to make the chimney taller than necessary so that the fireplace would draw well, so well that it would tug at the clothes of anyone who stood in front of it.

The second problem I faced was one of experience. I had never constructed a fireplace before. I had assisted a few times, certainly, but I had never tackled the entire set of complications alone. That was exciting but also somewhat intimidating.

I had something else in mind that morning as well. Looking around to make sure no one was watching, I stood in front of the cement mixer and studied it carefully. Then, taking a deep breath, I moved into position and grasped it by its steel harness. Exhaling and conjuring up a picture of Atlas in my mind, I exerted all the force of my back and legs, trying to get the enormous thing off the ground. It made noises—little creaks and whines—but it did not budge an inch. I rested and wondered if possibly António had been putting me on. He was playing a cruel joke on a poor, unsuspecting foreigner.

A voice from behind startled me. "Trying to lift the cement mixer?" It was Ba.

"Oh, no," I lied. "I just thought that maybe we should move it a bit here to the left. What do you think?"

"Don't bother hurting your back," Ba replied. "Only António can lift that thing."

I walked off with my head hanging down.

A few hours later my pride returned as I mitered the last few pieces of the fireback and set them into place. I wasn't sure if the fireplace would ever work, but it was certainly a thing of beauty. Paulo and Alberto wandered over to examine my efforts. What was it, they asked. And when I told them, they shook their heads. It won't work here, they said. This was Portugal. Things were different here. Didn't I want them to construct a typical fireplace?

No, I said. This one would be fine, I was sure. They went off to a corner, mumbled between themselves, then returned. We would make a bet, they said. If the fireplace really worked, they would take Barbara and me out to lunch. If it didn't, well then, we could take them. How did that sound?

After my failure with the cement mixer that morning, I wasn't about to back down. Agreed, I said, and we shook hands. They went off to tell António about the tasty lunch they were about to win for themselves, and I began to recalculate all the angles and dimensions of the work in progress. We had now entered the sphere of challenge, of competition, of stupid manly bets that pitted ego against ego. The fireplace had to work! Maybe I would put a fan in the chimney while they weren't watching.

A few days later, as Barbara and I were coming back to the cottage from a picnic lunch we had had on an adjacent hillside, we saw a remarkable sight. António, Paulo, Alberto, and Ba had returned from their lunch early—or, rather, on time. It had always been their habit to come back to work at about 1:20 or so. Paulo said they had to see the news and the soccer scores that came on television at 1:00. Today their motorcycles were piled in their usual heap, but there was no sign of them. Then I saw smoke coming from the rooftop. They were trying out the fireplace! We went into the living room to find the four of them huddled in front of the hearth, stoking a fire of twigs and scrap wood, and watching the smoke swirl and disappear up the chimney.

I couldn't resist. *"E então?"*

They all jumped to their feet, looking very embarrassed. "It seems to work," Paulo finally said.

"Yes, it does," I replied, "even though the chimney's not through the roof yet. It will draw even better then."

Alberto came forward and offered his hand. "Congratulations," he said.

Muttering, they ambled away, the last few minutes of their precious lunch hour squandered on a lost bet.

"And the lunch?" I asked in a casual voice.

Oh, yes, something would be worked out. Next week maybe. They wouldn't forget.

No, I thought, they wouldn't forget. I wouldn't let them.

Fruit Lady

22

IT WAS ON MY SEVENTH OR eighth trip to the *notário* that the miracle happened. After waiting for only an hour, I was called and began presenting all the requisite papers as usual, spreading them out on the desk. I was behaving in an ultra-polite manner and by now had learned the names of all the chirpy women who worked there. It was as if they were old friends. Once I had even brought them chocolates. On that occasion they had seemed genuinely distressed that my importation bulletin would expire before they could schedule me for the closing. Since then I had given up hope of ever having all the necessary papers in order and valid for the necessary length of time required to assemble everyone necessary to actually effect the sale and transfer of the cottage.

But today Joanna, the prettiest and perkiest of the group, skimmed over the papers quickly and put them in a neat pile. I smiled at her and asked what was missing this week.

"Nothing," she said. "I'm going to schedule you for *escritura.*"

I was truly shocked. Actually being scheduled for a closing had become like finding the Holy Grail for us, akin to winning a lottery or jackpot from a slot machine. Suspicious, I began to ask questions. "But what about the importation bulletin? Surely it must have expired?"

Joanna pulled it out from the pile and showed me a brief note written in pen on the bottom. "See that?" she said. "It says that the bulletin is good until *escritura* is over. They do that sometimes when the bulletin has been renewed several times. I guess they get tired of reissuing the same thing over and over."

So that was it, I thought. The key to getting anything done in Portugal was exhaustion. You simply had to keep plugging away until the authorities were so bored that they lost interest in you and would grant you whatever it was you were after. It was a simple but effective technique. Survival of the most persistent. Grind them down until their senses were dulled by your continual pleas. It made perfect sense. Those who continued to appear day after day to present their numerous papers obviously had an interest in accomplishing some task. Otherwise they would have given up after the first few futile tries. It was rather like the Napoleonic Code—guilty until proven innocent. And if by the time your case came to court you couldn't prove you were still damaged or injured, well then, obviously you had recovered sufficiently to no longer warrant the court's scrutiny. It was pragmatism at its most basic.

I exhaled a deep sigh of relief. A major hurdle had been crossed. Now if only the water company would come around, we might finally be able to move into the twentieth century.

Joanna was speaking to me. Was I all right? Would Thursday afternoon in two weeks' time be satisfactory? They could do it sooner, but the sellers' family was fairly extensive and everyone had to be notified.

Yes, yes, I mumbled. That would be fine—perfect, in fact. I kissed Joanna's hand in a moment of euphoria and backed out the door, bowing. I didn't care what they thought of me. We had a date for closing!

Ruined Cottage

23 AS USUAL IN LIFE, MANY
things happened during the two weeks we waited for the closing. For example, it was only two days after scheduling the
monumental event that an omen occurred, although we didn't
recognize it as such at the time. I had finally perfected my own
method for removing the old wall covering of mud, sand, and
lime. A flat shovel and a sledgehammer were my choices of in-

struments of destruction, and I had become quite adept at removing large chunks of this primitive plaster at a single go. I thought I had vastly improved on the Portuguese method of hammer and chisel, and was taking great delight in felling huge slabs, listening to the resounding crash they made when they hit the floor.

On this particular morning I was working on the upper floor in a room we had come to call the "landing," for lack of a better name. It was the rather extensive area at the top of the circular staircase bounded on both sides by bedrooms. I felt very energetic that morning. I had arrived early and actually got the cement mixer to wobble when I tried to lift it. Scheduling the *escritura* had given me renewed vigor, a healthier appetite, and curly hair. It had even made me more optimistic about dealing with the water company. I would use the same tactics with those bureaucrats, I thought—wear them away, gnaw at them until their spirits were too tired to resist any longer.

My soul was singing as I inserted the shovel into the small crack in the wall I had made with a hammer and chisel. Picking up the sledgehammer, I began to pound away on the shovel's handle, watching the flat blade disappear into the ancient plaster. Usually I could embed it two or three feet into the wall, loosen the plaster in the surrounding area, and then, exerting pressure on the shovel handle, pull it away from the rubble stonework beneath it. It was immensely satisfying work.

And this particular "run" was going very well. Already the shovel had sunk to the hilt—much further than I had ever been able to insert it before. A large chunk of plaster slowly began to detach itself from the wall. It seemed to be all too easy, I thought, but shrugged it off as a silly premonition. Then I got greedy. If I could pound the shovel in that far so easily, why not force it even farther into the wall, thereby freeing up an even larger chunk of plaster? With Olympic records in mind, I found a large crowbar and mated it to the end of the shovel, then began pounding on the end of that. It, too, began to disappear into the recesses of the plaster, and I noticed that the entire wall had begun to come loose. This was progress! Immensely proud of myself, I went to fetch António and Paulo to show them the fruits of American ingenuity.

They looked at the wall with alarm. What would happen to the wood floor when all that plaster fell on it, they asked. It was a tremendous amount of weight to come crashing down on a pine floor, especially one supported by ancient chestnut beams of uncertain engineering. True, I thought. I hadn't anticipated the force of the fall, but I had investigated the old beams with a drill to determine their sturdiness. Adrenaline was building, and my hormones told me to go for it. I warned them to stand back and took a few more swings with the sledge. Then, grabbing the crowbar firmly, I torqued it away from the wall.

Suddenly the entire wall came loose and slammed onto the floor. The house shook and reverberated, and an enormous cloud of dust billowed up through the room. António and Paulo began coughing loudly, Barbara shouted from below, and Alberto came running up the stairs. I could see nothing through the cloud of dust, and it was only after it began to dissipate that I suspected something was wrong.

António saw it first and let out a low whistle. There was no wall anymore! We were looking into the adjacent house. As the dust cleared I could make out particulars—an old iron bed with a chintz cover, a little bedside table now covered with a thick layer of dust, a peeling, painted armoire in a corner.

"*É da Dona China,*" António muttered. It was China's bedroom, plain and simple. I could see her family photos on the bedside table shrouded in dust. I certainly hoped she wasn't home. And what a great stroke of luck that she wasn't in bed!

Paulo figured it out first. "This was all one big room back when these two houses were one," he said, "before the sisters fought. After the fight they must have built this partition."

My mind was already on more pragmatic things. "What are we going to do?"

"Simple," Alberto said. "Buy the other house quickly, before *Dona* China comes home."

I stared at the huge opening in the wall, then moved through to China's side. Her house was very sparsely furnished, with only the most rudimentary objects necessary for existence. There were no chairs, no television, no refrigerator, I noticed, peering into the small cubicle she used as a kitchen. Just the essentials, some lace doilies, and the lingering smell of dust and Sintra mold.

"I wonder where she is," I said.

"She's down at the Salvation Army," António responded. "I saw her there on my way up."

"Maybe we could put the wall back up before she comes home," I said. "Give it a quick coat of whitewash, then come back and plaster it the next day she goes out."

The masons discussed the proposition, and Paulo volunteered for the job.

"Wait a minute," Alberto interrupted. "She had me over there yesterday to look at some work she wants done. I think I saw a padlock on her front door."

We all went around to her door to investigate. Sure enough, there was an antiquated padlock hanging on a sliding bolt. Bad luck. That meant there was no way to get in or out after we put up the new wall.

"We can still do it," Paulo said. "I can build the wall from her side, and before I put in the last few blocks, I'll paint the wall and have António lift me out of her room. I can paint the last couple of blocks and then slide them in from your side."

I agreed. It seemed to be the only solution. We could deal with getting in on her side to finish later.

Paulo began laying the blocks after they told Ba, who had been grooming the path in front of the cottage, what had happened. As Ba started to remove even more debris, António pulled me aside.

"More bad news," he said and motioned for me to follow

him into what was going to be the master bedroom. He pointed up at the edge of the ceiling.

"It's fallen about five centimeters."

I looked up and saw he was correct. A section of the ceiling was definitely sagging.

"Shouldn't be a problem," I said. "We'll just jack it up and screw it back into place."

António frowned. "I don't think so. The whole roof has to be redone."

"What!" That made me nervous.

"There's no alternative," António said. "These ceiling rafters support the roof beams, and the ceiling rafters are all rotten. I'm sure of it. In fact, it's probably dangerous just to be standing here now."

I couldn't believe it. "But I checked them before," I said. "They looked fine."

"Sure, they looked fine, but they're rotten inside the walls. And now with us hammering on the walls, they've started to break off."

"Well," I suggested, "why can't we just build another wall, a false wall inside the real wall to support the rafters where they aren't rotten?"

"It's possible," António said. "But think about the work. To build a wall up here on the upper floor you have to build another wall below on the ground floor to support it, right?"

He was correct. I hadn't considered that. A block wall around the upper-floor perimeter seated on a wood floor would certainly need support underneath, which would also mean building a perimeter wall around the ground floor—in essence building an entire new house inside the existing house.

My heart sank. Neither time nor budget would allow for the construction of walls or a new roof. Roofs were always high-profile items—time-consuming and expensive. And if this was the case in other countries, it was certain to be more so here in Portugal. And the added expense would surely put us over the edge. I stared up at the delicate stucco molding on the ceiling—the molding I had worked so hard to save. It would be lost now.

As I searched my mind for some alternative solution, we heard a commotion outside the bedroom window. There were several voices and the sound of feet. António and I both stepped to the window just in time to see several men passing in front of the cottage carrying a coffin.

António called out to the men and asked who had died. "The gentleman from over there," one of the pallbearers called back. He nodded his head in the direction of José and Lucinda's house. "One of the ancients."

António sighed and made the sign of the cross. "It's bad luck to work anymore today," he said. "Tell Paulo and Alberto I'm at the bar."

I went to look for Barbara to give her all sorts of bad news, not knowing quite where to start. I found her with Mathias, her problem pupil, doing watercolors near the village fountain. But rather than disturb her "therapy" session, I decided to seek my own form of solace and followed António down to the bar.

Neighbors

24 THE DAY OF THE CLOSING,
the *escritura,* the *notário*'s office overflowed into the street. I had
never seen it so busy. People were everywhere, elbowing each
other for position, gesticulating, shouting angrily in loud voices.
The only time I had seen so many people was at the water company, and as I gazed at their faces, I saw several that were familiar to me from my visits there. Perhaps it was a ritual that one

was required to perform, eternally circulating from office to office, bureaucracy to bureaucracy, attempting to put some simple life together, some rudimentary sense of harmony and order. I certainly knew the feeling.

I had made a date to meet Sara at a café near the notary's office so I didn't yet have to brave the crowd milling outside the doors. Sara was going to accompany me to the closing, and that helped calm my nerves. She had been to many closings and knew the ropes and all the notaries well, she said.

Barbara had elected not to come. With José's death just a few days before and the news about the roof repair, she had lost momentum. Buying a house we might soon have to sell didn't excite or interest her. She had decided to stay behind and work on her wall-stenciling.

I took a seat in the café and ordered warm *pasteis de natas* with cinnamon and a *galão,* or coffee with milk. It would do me well to sugar up for the events of the day, I figured, and as I sat waiting for Sara's arrival, I thought about our future in Portugal.

There was no doubt we loved the climate, the beauty, and the people. We had come to be accepted graciously in the village once we had established that we intended to actually live there rather than just spend a few summer months. And when it became known that I was intrepid enough to confront the water company, many of the villagers came to me with other problems—water pumps that didn't work, seeds that didn't sprout, prescriptions they could not read, or daughters with unwanted pregnancies. I attempted to deal with all these things with poise and equanimity, and obviously with varying success. Pumps I tapped with small hammers, seeds I threw away, prescriptions I put my glasses on to read, and daughters I referred to the local priest. It was good to feel needed no matter what the problem, and the villagers as a whole were a gentle and modest lot.

Still, we were rapidly reaching the end of our financial rope and would probably have to sell the cottage once we had finished renovations. But as I had reassured Barbara at length, selling the House of the Little Cats did not mean departure from the village. There were several other ruins for sale, and with the small profit we might make from finishing *Gatinhos* and putting it on the market, we could probably leap-frog into a more spacious "cottage." In fact, we might even have a bit more cash to spend on whimsy and caprice when decorating it. True, times would be rough until we sold *Gatinhos,* but it was going to be so charming, who could resist buying? She still did not seem overly encouraged, but I knew time would change that.

Thinking of time, I glanced at the café clock. Sara was late. The *escritura* was scheduled for 10:00 A.M., which left only five minutes to jostle my way through the crowd. Sara had said she would be here at 9:30. I could wait only a minute more.

I gulped down the last bit of pastry, paid the bill, and scanned the café one last time. No sign of Sara. Outside I saw that the throng had quieted down somewhat at the notary's office. I took a firm grip on my briefcase, empty as it was, and strode off in that direction. I joined the crowd at the bottom of the staircase that led up to the office, not knowing what to expect next. I decided not to try to break through the line, rationalizing that it might somehow jinx the carefully preplanned events of the day.

Then I heard a voice from above.

"Oh, *Senhor* Ricardo!"

It was the old man who had originally shown us the house, although I hardly recognized him, resplendent as he was in an oversized sport coat and slacks. He rushed down the staircase, pushing people out of the way, and gave me a massive bear hug. I commented favorably on his Western-style string tie and noticed that he reeked of cologne and pomade. He even seemed somehow to have polished up his two remaining teeth.

Whatever the circumstances, I was glad to see him again. I had come to trust the old man and quite enjoy his exuberance. It had taken me a few months, but I finally realized that he had really not misled us at all about the details of the cottage. He was simply of another age, another century, and we had come to appreciate his lack of guile.

"So," he said, "today is the great day!"

I replied that, yes, it had finally come, and we were certainly happy about that. We had begun to worry that it might never take place, this purchase of his house.

"Ha," he said with a laugh. "Not to worry. Everything happens in Portugal with time. It's just necessary to be patient."

I was beginning to learn that, I said. Had he seen Sara here by chance?

He clucked his tongue loudly and shook his head. No.

I thought of trying to call her but quickly realized that by the time I found a working phone and lined up all the little coins properly in the slot, one of my life's major rites of passage might be over. No, I would have to go this alone somehow, forge ahead slowly, Saint George confronting the dragon of bureaucracy. I decided to recruit the old man to help me.

"Is everyone here from the family?" I asked.

Yes, he said, almost everyone—except for Jorge and Leopoldina who were coming by train. The rest had taken all morning to round up, but they were here now. And it was a perfect time for me to meet them.

He introduced me to the couple standing next to him. I shook their hands and tried to commit their names to memory. Cousins, the old man announced, then proceeded to introduce me to another couple standing at the foot of the stairs. I greeted them and for some unknown reason thanked them for coming. All the while I was closely guarding my backside, in case a pickpocket might be lurking in the crowd, waiting for a chance to make off with the remainder of the house payment that I had been forced to bring in cash.

Standing at the very bottom of the winding stairs, the old man began to beat vehemently on the banister. The noisy crowd packed onto the staircase suddenly fell silent.

"*Atenção!*" The old man's voice seemed to squeak when he

spoke so loudly. "This is *Senhor* Ricardo, the buyer!"

The people began to whisper among themselves, and I asked the old man who they all were.

"Family," he replied. "And here comes Jorge and Leopoldina! Now we are all present."

I was dumbfounded. There must have been over forty people on the staircase and more behind us.

"All these people," I stammered. "They are all family?"

"Ha, ha," the old man laughed. "There are even more upstairs."

He must have seen the look of anguish on my face. *"Calma!"* he said. "Don't worry. Not all of them have to sign. Some are here only to watch and . . ." He rubbed two fingers together to make his point.

But the numbers made me panic. Where the hell was Sara? What was I supposed to do? It was already after ten.

A hush fell over the crowd again as the word was passed down that I was being summoned to the notary's office. Then, like the parting of the waters for Moses, a path opened up in the center of the staircase. My first thought was to flee. This was too frightening. There was too much money involved—all of our money.

But it was too late. The old man was already pushing me up the steps. I shook hands right and left as my panic mounted and the faces became a blur. On the landing outside the office I saw even more people waiting inside. I felt like a tender piece of meat being thrown to the lions.

"Pst! Pst!" It was the old man. He pulled me close. "Watch out for Prego. He's a bad one!"

And with that cryptic message, he pushed me inside.

I made my way slowly to Joanna's window and greeted her.

"You see?" she said. "I told you everything would happen sooner or later. Are you ready?"

I decided to be honest with her and told her I was extremely nervous. So many people.

"Well, I told you it was a big family. Sometimes it's like that."

"But there are seventy or eighty people here."

"But not all of them are here to sign," Joanna said. "Some are here just for the excitement. Like a bullfight. How many in your family?"

"Two."

"Well," she said, "they told me things were different in America. But don't worry about all the people. Your attorney will tell you what to do."

I cringed. "But I don't have a lawyer."

Joanna seemed surprised. "You don't?"

I told her no. I had planned on Sara coming.

"Sara? That English woman? She never comes."

Oh, perfect, I thought, balancing on the edge of mental stability. I was really alone.

Joanna said something about calling me in a moment, but I wasn't listening. I was too busy trying to calm my nerves. And as I attempted to slow down my pulse and breathing, using techniques I vaguely remembered from a Lamaze class I had once attended, someone tapped me on my shoulder. A short, squat, intensely ugly man was confronting me, and my first thought was that he might be an employee of the notary office. But any hope of that flew out the window when he dropped his cigarette to the floor and crushed the butt with his shoe. He stuck out his hand.

"*Bom dia.* My name is Prego."

Prego, I thought. Mr. Nail. The one the old man had warned me about. I shook his hand as firmly as I could under the circumstances.

"Nice to meet you," I said, not meaning a word of it.

"It's about the contract," he said.

"Yes?" I responded.

"It's not proper. It's not correct."

"Oh?"

"I'm a very important contractor in Lisbon. I deal with very large contracts all the time, and I can tell you your contract is no good."

There was something very intense about this man that I did not like at all. Maybe it was the way his eyebrows grew together over his warty nose. But his assertion and the way he made it worried me. I attempted humor. "Your name is Prego, 'nail,' and you're a contractor?" I said. "That's very handy, don't you think? Appropriate?"

He wasn't smiling. "I personally will not sign the deed," he said. "And I am going to tell the rest of the family that they should not sign, either."

I tried to look calm and collected but knew I was failing miserably. I searched for some way to counter his threat and found myself vaguely regretting the day I had ever begun to study the Portuguese language. To what end? Here I was alone and totally perplexed without a translator or lawyer in sight. Had pride or ignorance done this to me?

Mr. Nail spoke again. "Of course we might be able to work something out. Maybe I could overlook the errors of the contract. I might be able to do this."

That sounded encouraging. "Good," I said. "Thank you."

"If you gave me a little present for my son's education."

"Ah, you have children?" I said stupidly, trying to break down his resistance.

"No," he said with a scowl. "I don't have children. I hate children. One hundred fifty contos."

I shivered. He wanted 150 contos? That was $1,000! Impossible. We were flying so low to the ground right now that we would have been hard pressed to come up with $100. What to do then with Mr. Nail? Could he really upset this whole process? I suspected he could. And if he did, if the family reneged completely on the contract and was forced to pay back double the deposit and reclaim the house, they would still be winners in the end because of all the renovations we had already made.

Memories of the many horror stories we had heard floated through my mind—of people who had paid deposits to individuals who didn't even own the land they pretended to sell, of other foreigners who paid large deposits only to find out they could not legally buy the property they sought due to agricultural restrictions. Then there was a story about a Portuguese family who sold a house to foreigners and on the day of closing went there and removed every plant, scrub, and tree from the property.

I thought about everything that had happened since we arrived here, and it made me smile. It had been hard work shaping our psyches to conform to the Portuguese mold. We had learned many lessons and still had major hurdles ahead to forge a comfortable life. But again, the people, the climate, the air, the light, the Sintra mountains themselves—all had gradually carved out a spot in our hearts. We were even beginning to love chaos, to look forward to Sandra's parties, to relish António's latest excuse for a prolonged absence. We were not ready to relinquish all of this under any circumstance.

I stared Mr. Prego right in the eye. "I'm not going to give you any money," I said. "But what I will do is take you over to the café and buy you a coffee and maybe even a *bagaço*. Then if you still insist on extortion, Mr. Nail, I'm going to get a hammer and pound you into the ground."

Neither one of us could believe what I had just said. Prego ran the words through his small brain one more time and backed away from me. At the same moment a door opened, and someone called out my name along with several others, asking us to enter.

Prego stood in my way. "You're threatening me!" he shouted. "This man is threatening me!"

I walked around him, pretending not to hear him.

"This foreigner is threatening me!" he continued shouting. "I will not sign!"

I saw the old man across the room. He had witnessed

everything. He gave me a huge two-tooth smile, nodded, and chuckled loudly.

•

THE NOTARY'S OFFICE WAS LONG AND NARROW, AND SEVERAL CHAIRS strewn about were already occupied by members of the family. There was a small desk piled high with reams of disheveled documents and a grand assortment of rubber stamps. On the wall behind the desk was a large library of yellowing books. Two women were seated at the desk, and I was taking a position in a corner when a dispute erupted at the door. One of the women, a very attractive brunette, looked up and muttered under her breath, "Oh, no, it's going to be one of those."

She stood up and spoke in a loud voice. "Listen, please. Only twenty people can come in here. Only those people who have to sign should come in. If you're a spectator, you have to wait outside." She turned to the older woman seated next to her. "How many to sign?"

The older woman consulted a document. "Twenty-six."

The brunette, apparently the notary, spoke again. "Six of you will have to stand outside. We will call you when it's your turn to sign. And please be quiet!"

There was some commotion at the door, and I saw Prego elbow his way into the room. He walked directly to the desk and pounded on it with his fist. "I have been threatened!"

The young woman seemed surprised. "Oh? Who are you?"

Prego ran through a list of names too lengthy for me to follow. "I build big buildings in Lisbon," he declared.

The notary smiled, and I liked her immediately. "Which ones do you build? The ugly ones or the pretty ones?"

I noticed that the rest of the family seemed to be embarrassed by Prego's presence. They all were looking out the little window or else nervously wringing their hands.

Prego spoke again. "I build the ones that make me lots of money."

"That's very nice," the notary replied. "Now who threat-ened you?"

"The buyer!" he yelled.

"The buyer," she repeated. "Is the buyer here?"

I raised my hand meekly.

"Good morning," she said. She glanced down at the pa-pers, then confirmed my name. "You are . . ."

"Yes," I said.

"You're here alone?"

"Yes."

"No attorney. No translator?"

"No."

"That's unique. Do you speak Portuguese?"

"Some," I said. "A little. Sometimes."

"I see. Did you threaten this man?"

"I thought I offered to buy him coffee."

Prego interrupted. "That's a lie. He said he was going to pound me into the ground!"

I was beginning to feel more comfortable. The notary had obviously seen all this before. I trusted her.

"He wanted money," I said. "He demanded one hundred fifty contos."

The family gasped, and Prego glowered at me. It was al-ways bad form to mention specific monetary amounts, and it had the effect I had hoped for. Prego sought sympathy from the other members of the family but found none. They all glared back at him.

"I didn't ask for money," he said. "I only pointed out that the contract was not proper. I just—"

The notary held up her hand. "I've had enough of this. Go take a seat. If you want to object officially, you can do it later."

Prego walked away from the desk without saying a word.

"Now then," the notary said to the assembled crowd. "This man is about to give you a lot of money. Doesn't anyone want to offer him a seat?"

Immediately aware of this grave oversight, several people popped out of their chairs. I said that I was very willing to stand, but the notary pointed to the chair next to her desk. "Sit here. This is the buyer's chair."

One of the ancient uncles in a red beret leaped out of the chair and moved away, motioning for me to sit. I made my way forward. As I got closer I could smell the notary's perfume.

"We are going to read the documents now," she began after I was seated. "If there is anything you don't understand, you can stop us," she said to me. "And you," she said to Prego, "will be silent until I call you."

She glanced at the other woman, her secretary, obviously, and told her to begin. I was completely lost after the first sentence, so quickly did this woman tear through the legalese of the documents. I caught a familiar word here and there but finally decided to give up trying to understand. I would instead content myself by admiring the lovely notary. She caught me peeking at her once or twice but didn't seem to mind.

She stopped the reading at the end of a page and spoke to me. "How's it going?"

"Just fine," I lied.

She signaled the reading to continue, and it went on for another ten minutes. It was like listening to a Catholic mass in Latin.

"You have to listen carefully now," the notary said to me when the reading finally ended.

"No problem," I replied.

She went through the sales price, my name, my residence, the bulletin of importation of foreign funds, the papers from the fiscal office, my tax number, my application for residency, my exemption from SISA tax. All this I confirmed as best I could.

The notary then asked the family if they had been paid.

No one answered. They all just hung their heads.

She repeated the question, and I decided to answer. I told the notary that only the deposit had been paid and that I had the rest of the money in my pocket.

"You should pay the remainder now," she said.

I pulled the wad of bills out of my pocket. "Who should I give it to?"

Her eyes were open wide. "You brought cash?"

I explained that I had tried to get a certified check at the bank, but they told me that it would take twenty-four hours. I had no other option except to bring cash.

"All right, all right. Whose name is at the top?" she asked her secretary.

The other woman read off a name I recognized as the old man's. I heard him chuckling at the other end of the room.

"Give the money to the man making the strange noises," the notary said to me.

It was obvious that it would be difficult to reach the old man, so I simply handed the wad of bills to the person next to me and asked her to pass it on.

"No, no, no," the notary said. "Someone must confirm the amount before it starts traveling around the room. Otherwise . . ."

She didn't have to finish her sentence. The lady to whom I had handed the stack of bills immediately began to treat the money as if it were a hot potato, passing it to another woman on her left. This woman wanted no part of it, either. She withdrew her hand at the last second, and the money fell to the floor.

The notary tapped on her desk. "This will never do," she said. "Is this the way they do things in your country?" she asked me.

I replied I wasn't sure, but I didn't think so. Then I said there was really no problem. I knew several members of this family and trusted them. My words had an immediate effect, and everyone began to whisper. The lady next to me patted me on the back. I had obviously said the right thing.

The notary called them to order once again, then asked me to pick up the money and put it on her desk. She made the secretary count it and confirmed the amount with the old man. He clucked and said it was right.

All eyes turned as the money was passed down to him.

"Now," the notary said. "To sign. First is Philomena Duarte Saraiva. Are you here?"

The old man's wife rose and slowly made her way to the desk. There she paused, leaned over, and whispered to the notary.

"Get the ink pad," the notary told the secretary. "Very well. Who else can't write?" she asked the rest of the family.

This set off a noisy round of discussions, and a few minutes later the notary was banging on her desk again. "What is the problem now?"

The old man stood up and made a little bow. "Do you mean, Miss Notary, who can't write or who can't sign? Some of us can sign but we can't write. Like me, I can sign but writing—oh, oh, that's for another generation."

Most of those present seemed to concur.

"Well, you're next on the list," the notary said. "If you can sign, come and do it. I don't want an ink blob on the first line."

I was proud of the old man as he walked up to the desk. He smiled at me, stopped, touched the paper he was about to sign, then reached into his pocket and pulled out a case. Inside was a brand-new pen, which he carefully extracted and showed to the rest of the family. They were properly impressed, and I had to suppress an urge to applaud.

"Where?" he asked the notary.

The secretary showed him where to sign, and he bore down on the paper with gusto. His wife stood by his side and watched. A minute went by, and he was still writing. Then three more minutes. And another two.

By this time people were craning their necks trying to see what the old man was doing. Even I was perplexed. How many names could he have?

The notary finally broke in. "Stop," she said. "What are you writing?"

"I'm signing," the old man said.

The notary examined the document. "Have you ever signed anything before?"

"No," the old man said, "but I practiced all night to sign this."

"That's beautiful," the notary said, observing his handiwork. "But you took up four spaces."

"Want me to try again?" the old man asked.

"No," she said. "You can leave now."

The old man made his way out the door, stopping to shake my hand.

"Now," the notary said, "we're going to do it this way. Those who know how to write will sign next, followed by those who know how to sign but not how to write. Then we will fingerprint everyone else. All right?"

A general hum of consensus circulated through the group, then several family members stood, came up to the desk, signed, and left the room. Other family members filtered in, waiting their turn to sign. I was counting, and the deed had collected only eight signatures when there was a short pause and no one else came forward.

"No one else to sign?" the notary asked. "I mean, no others to sign who know how to sign?"

"I know how to sign." It was Prego speaking. "But I'm not going to."

The notary seemed perturbed. "All right," she said. "Let's talk about you. Prego, isn't it?"

Prego repeated his entire name in a haughty voice and even threw in a few titles.

"And you refuse to sign?"

"That's right."

"And you're going to tell us why now, aren't you?"

"The contract is improper. It's not correctly written."

"Oh?" The notary raised her eyebrows.

"Just look at my name. You see? Someone neglected to include my full name. It's an insult to me and my entire family."

"I'm so sorry," the notary said sarcastically.

"Well, it's very important for a man of my stature," Prego declared, "to always be called as he is known."

I could think of a few choice words for him but decided not to disturb the ceremony.

"And that's all you object to?" the notary asked.

"No, there's more," Prego muttered.

"How did I know that?" the notary said.

"Also, I was not properly notified," Prego said. "The letter I received was not on *papel selado*. It was on ordinary paper stock."

"I think it's a little late to protest that, don't you?" the notary said.

"I'm a very busy man. In fact, I have two hundred laborers waiting for me right now."

"Two hundred?" the notary repeated. "I'm very impressed. Listen, you have the right not to sign if you do not want to. If that is the case, the money must be returned immediately to the buyer as well as double the initial deposit, which is . . ."

She calculated the amount and announced it.

"You will also be liable as well for today's *escritura* fees. Let me see, that comes to eight hundred contos, more or less. Would you please put the money here on my desk now? Either cash or certified check is acceptable."

She began to tap her fingers on the desk. Prego shifted nervously from foot to foot. In a rising chorus the family began to attack him with modulated insults.

"Well," the notary said, "is someone going to pay?"

The family became more vehement, shouting at Prego to sign. He pulled out his wallet for a moment but stuck it back in his pocket. Then he strode angrily to the desk, picked up a pen, signed, and threw the pen down again.

"This is not right!"

The notary looked at his signature. "Thank you, Mr.

Prego. You will leave now. Please don't plan on coming to Sintra to build your buildings."

Prego turned red and began to say something. But the notary cut him off, and he indignantly stomped out of the room.

"Now those who can sign their names next, please."

A few more people got up and signed the deed. One of them apologized for Prego's behavior. "It's not a problem," the notary said. "It happens every day. It's good you didn't pay him," she remarked to me.

"I didn't have a choice," I said.

"All right," she continued. "Now everyone who can't sign."

The secretary had the ink pad ready, and the first several fingerprintings passed without incident. Some of the people apologized, and others said that indeed they could sign but this was easier and more expedient.

Suddenly the secretary let out a loud scream. I looked over to see what had happened and noticed that she held—or, rather, was trying to hold—the hand of a woman who was missing three fingers.

"I'm sorry," the secretary apologized. "I wasn't expecting . . ."

"It was a car accident," the woman said. "We were coming down from vacation in the Minho when . . ."

She began an elaborate description of an accident that could happen only here in Portugal, one in which at least several parties were negligent quite apart from having absolutely no idea how to drive a motor vehicle. I was intrigued to finally hear an explanation for one of those mystery accidents, but the notary interrupted. "We must move on," she said. "There are others waiting."

The room began to clear somewhat, and the remaining "signers" lined up in single file. There was only one minor quandary when a cousin seemed to have no prints on his fingers. After brief questioning it was discovered that he worked at an acid factory. The notary pondered the problem for a moment, then said he should just put an X over the blank ink blobs he had made on the deed.

Finally everyone was gone. The notary held up the deed and scrutinized it. "This is the dirtiest deed I've ever seen. Oh, well. You get to sign, too," she said to me. "Or would you prefer to do a fingerprint?"

I picked up a pen and glanced down at the deed. It was truly a mess.

"Sign anywhere you want," the notary said. "I don't think it matters anymore."

I found a tiny space near the bottom of the page and signed my name. Then I stood, paid the fees, and thanked the notary profusely for her assistance.

"It's my job," she said. She congratulated me on the purchase of the house. "But are you really sure you want to live here?" she asked. "In this silly little third-world country?"

"Oh, yes," I replied. "Where else can you have an adventure like this?"

"I see," she said. "Perhaps you can write a book about it."

I took note of her suggestion.

"By the way," she said, "your contract was a piece of garbage. You're lucky the family was honest. If you're foolish enough to do this again, get a lawyer or at least a *solicitador*."

I said I would and thanked her again. On my way out I shook Joanna's hand, then, exhausted, started down the stairs. At the ground level I saw a large group of people standing just outside the door. It was the family. What were they still doing here?

When I walked out into the sun, they began to cheer, clap, and pat me on the back.

"Good luck," they all said as they shook my hand in turn. "You'll need it here."

Azenhas Do Mar

25

WAS IT BENJAMIN FRANKLIN
who said that fish and guests begin to smell after three days? In
our experience, forty-eight hours seemed to be the threshold
beyond which hospitality began to take on the proportions of
burden and breakdown. Any longer period of enforced proxim-
ity always seemed to disintegrate into a struggle to maintain the
basic components of civility.

Barbara and I had considered the problem of guests at length. When we first announced we were moving abroad, we were immediately besieged by acquaintances who offered to "drop in" just to keep us in touch with reality. They would ensure that we didn't "go native," they said. We recognized most of these offers for what they were—vague threats that would never be carried out, made by people who rarely ventured beyond their city limits. There were a few occasions, however, when someone slipped through our protective net or when a couple we had met only briefly suddenly appeared and announced they had arrived to take us up on our "invitation."

Our first visitor was Barbara's brother, affectionately known as "Pom." Although he swore he had come to work with us, he had packed only slacks and sports coats. He was certainly amiable enough, but every night he insisted on dragging us to cutting-edge discos guarded by gargantuan bouncers. Barbara, master of Portuguese that she was, taught him to say, "Hello, I'm lonely" and "Would you like to dance?" Unfortunately, one night Pom got a little drunk and attempted to corner a number of "discoettes," chanting his rudimentary Portuguese invitations. By the time we arrived to rescue him, the Lisbon police had poor Pom all tied up until he looked like Houdini about ready to perform his act.

Other visitors came and went with little trouble until just a few weeks after the *escritura*. We were concentrating on building the roof, and Barbara and I were confronting the fact that we had to sell the house we had just bought and had become very attached to when Constance arrived. Constance was possibly a friend of Barbara's—Barbara was not quite sure because she had experienced a brief period of madness when she invited absolutely everyone she met to come and spend years with us in Portugal. She had stopped issuing such invitations after I pointed out the real danger that some of these people might actually appear. The time was not right for that yet. We would be involved in settling in, renovating a house. Capricious visits during the early months of our stay would only hinder our efforts to complete the project and actually move in. Later, perhaps, there would be time for open-ended entertaining and the leisure to revisit castles and palaces and retell the history of our adopted homeland.

When Constance's letter arrived announcing her intention to pay us a visit, Barbara seemed to remember that she had met her at a women's gathering of environmental conservationists. She had taken notice of her, Barbara thought, because she was bouncy and bright. Constance was a therapist, a licensed psychologist, she recalled. She must be okay, Barbara said. She was emotionally and environmentally correct. What else was there?

We had begun to discuss Constance seriously when we received her second letter. Many people had written us letters asking when it would be a good time to "drop in." We had answered them simply and truthfully that it was not a good time for a visit right now and even told them they should contact us again in a few months when things would be more auspicious. We never heard from most of these people again. Constance, on the other hand, had written back a very sympathetic letter, saying that she was aware of the pressures we must be under but she could help us resolve them. Not only that, her letter stated, but she would also be able to help us finish the house since she had just completed a renovation project of her own.

To this we had replied with profuse and false gratitude. How very kind it was for her to think of us and even offer to help, but right now it was just not possible. We had no extra bedroom or bed, and our funds were running precariously low. Perhaps she could come in September? Two weeks later she called us from the airport asking for a ride. But hadn't she received our last letter? No, she said, she hadn't, but she thanked us for confirming her plans anyway.

It hadn't been a particularly pleasant morning. The municipal sanitation truck had finally appeared, after repeated requests, to pump out an ancient cesspool we had discovered in the center of the garden. The men had almost finished the task when their large hose ruptured, sending a slurry of malodorous black liquid flowing down through the village.

That immediately set off a chorus of protests, of course, which ended only when Barbara and I requested permission from Poncho, the famous architect who lived in the village, to use his hose and private well water to wash down the streets and alleys. We were just finishing that fetid task when word arrived of Constance's call.

We both willingly quit work, bathed, and took off for the airport. There was an unspoken principle between us that we would provide hospitality for anyone who asked for it. We had been sheltered many times throughout the world and had decided that we would do the same for others. Constance had somehow slipped through our line of defense. Now that she was here, however, she was our guest, for better or worse.

We greeted her affectionately at the airport, loaded her several suitcases into our van, then did a little sightseeing. Constance, young and attractive, seemed to drink it all in with relish. She had never been abroad before, she said. And this was just perfect for her. My heart sank.

We drove briefly through Sintra and actually stopped for tea at Hotel Seteais, the most luxurious hostelry in the area. When we arrived back at the cottage, we introduced Constance to the crew as one of our dear friends, and everyone, with the exception of António who was off crushing grapes, bowed and ogled her with interest.

We showed Constance around the cottage, which now had a skeleton of roof rafters in place, wood that had been cut and milled locally to our specifications. We showed her Barbara's famous arch, my Rumsford fireplace, and the gracefully molded gateway I had built with a flower box on top. We pointed out the "little cat" ceramic tiles we had found to commemorate the name of the cottage. We unveiled the ornate cast-iron staircase I had finally managed to wrestle into place. And we explained about the problems of removing debris, another huge pile of which had accumulated due to the demolition of the roof. We told the tale of breaking through the wall into China's house and how we had tried to cover up our tracks by offering to do small renovations on her cottage, thus giving us access to the wall, which we had finally managed to plaster properly and re-paint. We went into some detail because she had offered to help in her letter. We hoped there would be some aspect of the project that she would latch onto and make her own.

Constance looked it all over and pronounced her satisfaction with our efforts. Then she asked where the nearest beach might be. When we arrived back at Mummy's flat, she unpacked nothing but vacation wear. And no, she said, she had absolutely no objection to sleeping on the fold-out couch in the living room.

And so a new routine began. I would get up early, go to the job site, and attempt to lift the cement mixer before anyone arrived. Barbara would come later and announce that Constance was ready to be taken to the beach. I would then leave the job site and drive her to the beach, setting a time when I would leave work again and pick her up. Of course I resented the arrangement, but it seemed to keep Constance happy enough. Besides, she and Barbara were going through the rituals of female bonding, which I thought must be good. I didn't say much at first because Constance was a therapist, and I hesitated to express my true feelings, afraid she might label me dark and disturbed or worse.

We quickly discovered, however, that—horror of horrors—Constance's stay was open-ended. It seemed she was going through some sort of crisis with her husband, who was going through some sort of crisis of his own. We called it the "domino crisis effect" because after only a few days their crisis became our crisis.

It all began simply enough one evening. I was making dinner at Mummy's while Barbara and Constance communed over coffee at the café around the corner. I heard the front door open and then slam shut, and Barbara appeared in the kitchen, obviously upset.

"I don't believe it!" she said and began to pace the floor.

I put my parsley chopping on hold and asked her what was wrong.

"Her. Constance. She accused me of being just like her husband!"

"I see," I said, shutting off the burner under the curried chicken. "Her husband. Is he a bad guy?"

"He's a recovering abusive alcoholic."

"She accused you of that?"

"No, she accused me of being obsessive-compulsive."

"Well, she is a therapist," I said.

"Yes, but she's our guest. Life is hard enough without having someone you're feeding point out your inadequacies."

"I warned you about guests."

"And spending every day on the beach," Barbara continued. "I don't believe it."

"I thought you said you were jealous?"

"Not anymore."

We both fell silent as we heard the door open. Constance came into the kitchen, and with what seemed to be practiced expertise, she made direct eye contact with both of us.

"I want to apologize," she said. "I haven't been very kind. It's just that I left a very strenuous situation at home." She stared down at the floor. "And here, when I try to relax, I have flashbacks. I'm sorry, Barbara."

They embraced. I whistled like Muzak and turned on the chicken again. A full moon rose in the evening sky.

"Oh," Constance said, "I saw that big fat guy who sometimes works for you at the beach. He said he would be there tomorrow."

António at the beach? I had to ask: "What was he doing?"

"Well, besides drinking, he was building sand castles."

Sand castles, I thought. And he had told us he would be slaughtering pigs.

Our dinner table conversation revolved around Portuguese drivers. Barbara ventured her opinion that a certain roundabout in Cascais was the epicenter of all bad driving in Portugal and that maladroitness behind the wheel radiated out from this point in ever increasing waves. She then related the true story of an American woman who had had an accident not too far from this intersection. The woman had been proceeding along peacefully when she was suddenly struck broadside by a vehicle that had run a stop sign. She got out of her demolished car with only minor injuries and began to harangue the other driver, a Portuguese woman, about failing to heed the stop sign. The Portuguese woman, not flinching, simply stated that there was no stop sign. The American woman pointed to the sign and asked, What was that then? Steadfast, the other woman continued to insist that the sign did not exist.

Both women exchanged insurance information, and the next day the American put in a call to her agent. He checked his computer and found that the Portuguese woman had not reported the accident to her company as was required to assess fault. He would look into it, he said.

The next day he called back to say that he had visited the site of the accident and that, indeed, there was no stop sign there. The American woman protested and said she would meet the agent at the spot in an hour. She arrived to find the stop sign gone without a trace. There was nothing left but a hole in the ground.

Exasperated, she went to the municipal building and requested the records concerning traffic signals and signs. She was told there were no records. A certain man, now retired, had been given the task of placing signs and signals where he saw fit many years ago. Perhaps she should go speak with him?

The story went on, and Barbara told it well. Then I added

my anecdote about the first taxi driver we had encountered in Lisbon who, when we asked him why he continually ran red lights, replied that the lights were not there to regulate traffic. No. Stop lights existed merely to assess blame should an accident occur.

After dinner we all went off to bed, but I awoke about an hour later thinking I had heard noises coming from the living room. Then I heard the front door of the apartment open and close quietly. Looking out the window, I saw Constance, dressed in her overcoat, heading away from the house. She had my flashlight in her hand and was walking up the road with purposeful strides.

Where in the world could she be going in the middle of the night? It was really none of my business, I thought. She was an adult, and it wasn't New York City. She was perfectly safe. I shrugged and went back to bed.

The next day, chauffeuring her to the beach, I jokingly accused Constance of having an affair.

"What do you mean?" she asked.

I told her I had heard her go out the night before and said I thought it was great that she had met someone. What were vacations for anyway?

She was silent for a moment, then said, "It's not that at all. It's not what you think."

"Oh" was all I could manage to say. What was going on then? Was she a cat burglar? A jewel thief? My imagination ran wild.

"I was feeding the dog," she said finally.

"The dog?" I asked. "What dog?"

"Pilote," she said.

Pilote was the dog that lived in China's yard next to her outhouse. It was not China's dog at all but had been left there by one of her nephews. As the story went, Pilote had bitten the postman several years ago, and the Guarda Nacional Republicana, the supreme authoritative entity in these matters, had given Pilote's owner an ultimatum: Put the dog to sleep or keep him restrained. Choosing the latter, the nephew had chained the dog in China's yard and made some kind of agreement with her. China had often joked that she kept the dog only because the nephew brought it good food, which she ate when he wasn't looking.

Barbara and I were indignant when we first heard the story. The fat little basset hound seemed friendly and innocuous enough. We played with him; the children of the village played with him. It seemed a shame to keep him chained up all the time. But if the Guarda found him on the loose, China said, they would shoot him and fine the owner an enormous fee. Pilote had a long chain and was free to roam the yard. Wasn't that better than dozing off to dog heaven? she asked. The postman had deserved to be bitten anyway. He was stupid and could never deliver letters to the right houses. They found out later that he couldn't read or write.

Pilote didn't look as if he was starving to me, but apparently Constance felt sorry for him. "It's not right," she said, "keeping him chained up like that."

When we arrived at the beach, I helped Constance unpack her towels and various other sundries. It was a glorious day at Praia das Maçãs. Multicolored cabanas lined the water's edge, topless bathers were lounging in the fine, pearly sand, and a squad of ambulatory merchants, all dressed in white, were hawking everything from pillows to cod croquettes. The beach itself formed a neat triangle, its apex the Colares River, which flowed lazily along the south side of the low ocher cliffs across from the village. Every fall the river flooded the beach with apples from upstream orchards, hence its name "Apple Beach." There was a jumble of cafés along the sea, a discotheque that didn't open until 10:00 P.M., and a tiny makeshift cinema that projected movies on a tautly stretched bedsheet.

I really didn't see any harm in giving Pilote food, I told Constance as I laid her supplies on the warm sand. In fact, if she liked, Barbara or I would be happy to feed him during the day to save her the walk in the middle of the night.

Constance said thank you, but she didn't mind the walk. She was having a hard time sleeping anyway.

Back at the cottage I got to work sheathing the roof. In defiance of the masons' pleas, we had decided on a wooden roof instead of the masonry affair they proposed. Wood was more authentic and typical. It was also less expensive and quicker. Wood was something I understood well. We had ordered some beaded tongue-and-groove boards for the sheathing. It would make a nice exposed ceiling, we thought. Elaborate stucco configurations were no longer an option on our new budget, which was really no budget at all. I had assumed the responsibility of putting down the boards since it involved the use of a power saw, and no one else would touch the tool.

I liked being up on the roof. The view over the valley and out to the ocean was splendid. I could see the farmworkers at Quinta de Vinagre spraying the grapevines from bright brass pump-packs on their backs. The vines were already heavily foliated, and small grape clusters had formed and were dangling from the trellises. Just beyond the vineyards, the Colares River, lined with ancient linden trees, shimmered in the midday sun. The surrounding hills were plush green now, and thick carpets of wild grass grew high on any spot where the forest didn't intrude. The sun was warm, and the fragrant smells of late spring seemed to be more intense.

As I worked, I stopped frequently to observe the daily rituals of the village. The roof was a perfect vantage point, and I could look down into backyards and windows otherwise invisible from the ground. I could see Isabel now, our neighbor to the west, busy over her cement washboard, pounding and pulling dirty shirts through gray soapy water. Further on I viewed the ladies of the village gathered at the fountain, filling their pitchers slowly as they discussed the state of the world with great animation. José and Lucinda's house, below, looked sad and unkempt, I noted. Lucinda wanted to stay on alone after José's death, but relatives had insisted she move in with them until her initial grief had passed. We deeply missed her ancient, cheerful face and her compliments about our construction efforts.

I finished nailing off an entire section of the roof and looked over into China's yard. Maybe it was just my imagination, but I was sure that Pilote had not budged from his prone position all morning. Of course, I had never observed him for extended periods before. Maybe he always spent his days sleeping. But just to allay my fears, I went over to visit him after lunch. He certainly wasn't at the gate to meet me, which was his habit when he heard someone approach. In fact, I noticed as I closed the gate behind me that he still hadn't moved from his earlier position.

Kneeling over him I could see that he wasn't dead. His breathing was very slow but regular, and his breath was as rancid as ever. I put my hand down and shook him. At first he didn't respond, but after continued proddings he finally managed to open an eye. It was a glazed eye that didn't seem to focus. I wasn't sure what was wrong with him but felt somehow responsible. I brought his water dish over to him and tried to get him to drink. I noticed small pieces of yellow chicken in his bowl. Constance really had been here and had even brought him the remnants of our dinner. Curry probably wasn't that good for a dog, but then it shouldn't have made him catatonic, either.

I got Pilote to drink a little water before he dozed off again. I would check on him later, I thought. But by the end of the day his condition hadn't changed. And Barbara, when she finally arrived, shared my concern about the dog, especially after I told her about Constance's nocturnal mission of mercy. We both resolved to speak to her that evening.

We went out to dinner that night at Senhor Gil's, a small communist restaurant that specialized in cheap grilled chicken. The restaurant consisted of several rickety tables inside a very plain block-walled lodge. The tables were covered with paper cloth on which sat oil and vinegar cruets and a large box of toothpicks. Gil, the owner, was making his rounds in a frayed cashmere sweater, greeting all his patrons personally, while the smell of sardines and wood smoke drifted into the dining room from the outdoor kitchen.

Once we were settled in and had wine and bread in front of us, we put the question to Constance. What exactly had she given Pilote to eat?

"Why?" she asked coldly.

I described Pilote's condition of extreme lethargy and our concern that he didn't seem at all well.

Constance looked away for a moment, distracted.

"It's just not right," she said, "keeping a nice little dog like that chained up his entire life. It's like he's on death row." Her eyes clouded over, and suddenly she began to cry. "I just wanted to help," she mumbled.

We tried to comfort her; Barbara put her arm around her shoulder, and I told her over and over that it was all right. It was a noble thing she wanted to do. No harm had been done.

Then she surprised us both. "I just gave him half of a Valium. I thought it would calm him down."

I was so shocked, I jumped out of my seat. Gil came running. Was everything all right? he inquired. Did we need more wine?

We pacified Gil with compliments, and he retreated, adjusting his thick glasses. Constance was sobbing into her third or fourth paper napkin. Barbara shrugged helplessly, and I was still incredulous. "You gave Pilote Valium?"

"Just a half," Constance said. "Crushed up in your curry."

"But do you give your dogs Valium in the States?" I asked.

"It's a prescription drug in the States," Constance replied. "Here you can get it over the counter."

She was right. It was perfectly true. The Portuguese loved pills, and they were all available to anyone who knew their names. Yet there was little apparent abuse. I related this to my alcohol theory: There was very little alcohol abuse by minors in Portugal since they were not forbidden access to it by law. It was an accepted part of life, not a "forbidden fruit," and it wasn't sought out as it was in countries that tried to regulate it.

Dogs and Valium—that was another matter.

"Do you have any more?" Barbara asked. "Maybe you should take one. Maybe we should all take one."

Constance stopped crying and glared at Barbara. "You see! You're just like him! That's exactly what he would say."

"I was joking," Barbara stammered defensively.

"No, you weren't!" Constance said and began to cry again.

When our chicken finally arrived, I made sure to check mine carefully for any signs of white powder.

Sintra

26 THE FOLLOWING DAY,

after again taxiing Constance to the beach, I set off for Sintra. With the success of the *escritura,* I no longer had to go from one office to another and felt I could now turn all my energy toward our main nemesis, the water company. It just so happened that on the same day I had submitted our petition to that divine body, I had also made an appointment with the president of the municipality. A reasonable person, I had assumed that the water company would take action in the interim. But, contrary to all reason, nothing had been done.

So on the appointed day I dressed up in my one and only sports coat and a fairly clean pair of slacks, then headed off for my appointment with the area's chief elected official. I knew nothing about the man at all—only his title. But I thought that as the mayor he would surely have leverage over a municipal entity. As I saw it, the main function of his office would be to correct any injustice suffered by citizens under his jurisdiction.

I had never been inside the municipal building, but I had admired the exterior for its lavish embellishments, the gargoyles and brightly tiled roof. I had wondered at this juxtaposition of fantasy and bureaucracy. Just how well did they coexist? My first intimation should have been the guard at the door. Although I had come to accept the presence of uniformed guards in the most unusual places, I never fully fathomed the need to protect incompetent engineers and minor elected officials.

Inside the building there was a central courtyard with a fountain, for some reason now dry. The space was full of sun and De Chirico–like shadows. The various offices on the ground floor were labeled with little plaques indicating their particular function. I spotted the one I wanted—Presidente da Câmara Municipal—went to the door, and turned the handle. The door did not open; the handle merely rotated in my hand. I immediately diagnosed the problem. The set screw was missing from the handle mechanism. Hoping to earn immediate accolades, I found a paperclip in my briefcase, manipulated it into the shape required, and inserted it into the screw hole. The door opened and swung inward.

I entered to find a small anteroom with a desk and a woman behind it with a horrified look on her face. She spoke without greeting me. "How did you get in here?"

I took the time to greet her, then explained the door's disfunction, offering to correct the problem if she would like.

She was still nervous. "How did you get past the guard?"

"I walked," I said. "He was busy reading the soccer paper."

I told her I was here for my appointment with the mayor, but the woman raised her hand. To see *Senhor Presidente,* she informed me, I had to have an official form with a fiscal stamp. The form was available on the second floor, but to get the stamp I would have to go into the center of town. She checked her watch. And if I went into the center of town, she continued, I couldn't possibly return in time for my appointment. Would I like to reschedule?

No, I said. I would take care of it. I went out the door, carefully closing it behind me. The fiscal stamp was no problem. In my briefcase I still had a large collection of stamps for every occasion. But when I ran up the stairs to the second floor, I discovered there were at least twenty people standing in line. With only five minutes to make my appointment, something drastic was in order. I went out of that office and ducked into the neighboring one where there was no line. Engaging the woman there in a strained casual conversation, I managed to learn the name of one of the women who worked behind the counter of the office next door.

Thus enlightened, I went back to the crowded office and called out the woman's name, Camilia, in a loud voice. After a moment she responded, and circumventing the line, I went directly up to her window. In a mixture of broken English and Portuguese I explained what I needed and added that the president himself had given me her name and was waiting for me now in his office. She nodded, signed a piece of paper, stamped it, and asked for a fiscal stamp. I opened my briefcase and brought out my array of stamps, which brought several sighs of admiration from those around me. With the stamp attached to the proper form, I ran back downstairs, feeling only moderately guilty.

At the president's office I turned the door handle again. It didn't open. The paperclip I had inserted was gone. I knocked forcefully several times, but there was no response. Repeated shouts produced the same result. I was beginning to feel somewhat unwelcome—and suspicious. Was it possible that the president's office operated under the same strictures as the water company?

Then came a stroke of good fortune. The door opened to let someone out, and before the man could cross the threshold, I darted in front of him into the office.

The secretary was appalled. "I told you, you cannot see the president without a certified form with a fiscal stamp."

I produced the piece of paper and handed it to her with a flourish.

After regarding it for a moment, she laid it down on her desk. Then she picked up a huge ledger and thumbed through the pages, finally stopping near the end of the book. She tapped the page with her finger. "Your appointment has been rescheduled," she said.

"Oh?"

"Yes. Let me see." She then announced a date eleven months in the future.

"No, thank you," I said and began to walk toward the only interior door. The woman kept talking behind me, saying something about how in reality today's appointment was only an appointment to make an official appointment later. Ignoring her, I went through the doorway into another vestibule and ran head-on into the largest Portuguese I had ever seen. Actually, António might have been bigger, but it was impossible to tell since this fellow was dressed in a loose-fitting suit. Our collision caused me to drop my briefcase, and as I stooped to pick it up, the man addressed me: *"O que é que o senhor quer?"*

"Can you lift a cement mixer alone?" I asked impulsively.

The man gave me a look as if I were totally insane.

"Actually, I'm here to see the president," I said.

"Huh!" he snorted, tugging at the fringe of his suitcoat. "About what?"

I showed him a copy of our petition to the water company and told him that I represented the entire village and not just myself. Glancing at it briefly, he threw it down on a small desk on one side of the room.

"The president's not seeing anyone today," he said, rubbing his hands together. "He's busy."

My time also had value, I protested, and if the president wanted to cancel appointments he should alert people in advance, using the telephone numbers one was required to leave when making an appointment. And by the way, he might get his door fixed before someone broke it down.

The man towered over me, blocking my way. So I really wanted to see the president?

"Absolutely," I said.

"How bad?" he asked. "How badly do you want to see him?"

Who was this man anyway? I finally asked, probably naively, exactly what he meant.

He shrugged, indicated a chair on one side of the room, and told me to sit down and think about it.

I did, my anger mounting. I considered going back to the cottage and returning with António. After all, he disdained authority as much as I did. But António hadn't shown up that day.

Meanwhile, the man had seated himself on the desk and was busy reading a soccer journal—the same one the guard had been reading at the door. They must have a multiple subscription, I thought.

I waited for half an hour. No one entered or left the office, and all was very quiet. I finally got up and went to the outer office. The woman was still sitting there, leafing through a sheaf of papers. "So," she said when she saw me. "Do you want to reschedule?"

"Not at all," I said. I was just curious about who this man in the other office might be.

The president's secretary, she replied.

I said I thought that she was the president's secretary.

"He has several," she responded. "He is very busy."

"Of course, of course," I mumbled. "But why is he so big?"

"The president is a very important man," she replied, "and so has many enemies."

And he was making another one right now, I thought. So the man was a bodyguard. The mayor of an area with thirty thousand residents needed physical protection. If they were all treated as I was being treated, I could understand why.

Just then there was a knock on the door, and the woman stood up and went to open it. So that was the secret. You had to knock without trying the handle to gain admittance.

A man entered and strode past me, but I managed to reach the doorway to the inner office in time to see him greet the bodyguard and slip him several bills.

Of course, you had to bribe your way into an audience. Corruption pure and simple. But I wasn't about to pay a bribe, so I quickly devised a plan. I took a sheet of paper out of my briefcase, ripped it up into several strips, and wrapped them inside a single one-hundred-escudo note. With this in hand, I walked toward the mayor's office door.

The bodyguard saw me coming and put down his newspaper. As he got up to meet me, I thrust out the disguised handful of paper. He took it from me, and I opened the door to the mayor's office. I was almost inside when I felt a viselike grip on my shoulder.

"*Heh pa, o que é isto!*"

The bodyguard pulled me back and displayed the worthless pile of paper. I was really mad now, and I gave him a good push that caught him off balance. He reeled back a few steps, tripped on a chair, and fell to the floor. The building shook. Fortunately the commotion attracted spectators to the scene, and they restrained the bodyguard from attacking me. In fact, it even brought the mayor out of his office.

He was a tall, extremely handsome man with flowing gray hair. He looked more like a French movie star than a Portuguese bureaucrat—but then wealthy families everywhere never looked like the poorer constituents of their countries.

The mayor demanded to know what was going on, and I launched into a detailed description of what I had had to endure to approach his office. I told him about the bribe, and he smiled when he saw the torn pieces of paper on the floor. The bodyguard then began his own dissertation with grunts and grumbles but was silenced by the mayor.

"I can tell by your accent that you're American, correct?" he said to me in flawless English.

Surprised at his fluency, all I could answer was Yes.

"Well," he said in a very paternal tone, "let me explain something to you. When you go to a Catholic church, you tithe, and you expect miracles, right?"

I nodded, transfixed.

"Well, here you may tithe also," he said, "but the miracles really happen. So why don't you just tell me your problem, and I will solve it. How does that sound?"

•

DRIVING BACK TO THE COTTAGE, I WAS VERY OPTIMISTIC. AFTER LIS-tening to the plight of the village and looking at our petition, the mayor had cursed Conception and her cohorts, and denounced them as procrastinators and water mongers. He would take care of the situation immediately, he said. Copious water would be flowing in a matter of days.

Unfortunately, my elevated mood didn't last long. I had just parked the blue van and was walking down to the cottage when I met the glum-faced crew headed for the bar.

"What's wrong?" I asked. "No one hurt, I hope."

António, who must have arrived after my departure, answered. "Worse than that. Ba is gone."

I got the whole story after buying two rounds at the bar. It seemed that Ba had been very nervous over the past few days. No one knew why. He was just like that, they told me. But this morning had been different. For some unknown reason Pilote, China's dog, was sick. He didn't move at all but just lay on the ground and howled out of the side of his mouth. The villagers, when consulted, said that he had made noise all night and had kept them awake.

"Probably dying," José, the bartender, interjected.

I knew better and gave serious thought to killing my first therapist.

The story continued. Ba had become increasingly agitated by the dog's howling until finally he burst out crying, threw down his shovel, and ran off into the woods.

I thought his behavior very strange and said so. After all, Ba was over sixty years old.

"But very sensitive," António said. "Like me."

Paulo and Alberto laughed. But during a lull in our conversation I could hear Pilote's plaintive howls, and I cursed all tourists everywhere. I thought sadly about Ba's departure and how it would affect the project. I had grown fond of Ba and certainly appreciated his work ethic.

"Maybe he'll come back," I said.

"No," António said. "He's done this several times. He never comes back."

I tried to lighten the mood and described my morning at the municipal offices. They all hung on my every word until I reached the part about my brief but personal encounter with the mayor himself.

"The mayor?" Paulo asked suspiciously. "A tall guy with silver hair?"

"Yes," I replied.

"I see," Paulo said. "Did he tell you he would take care of everything? In a few days even? Did he tell you not to worry?"

"Oh, no," I whispered under my breath, fearing the worst.

"He tells that to everyone who finally gets to see him," Paulo said. "He's the biggest *cabotino* in the country."

When we arrived back at the cottage, I immediately went for my English-Portuguese dictionary. *Cabotino* was a word I hadn't heard before, but there it was in the dictionary: *cabotino*—a buffoon, clown, hypocrite.

Paulo Setting Tiles

27

SEVERAL DAYS LATER THE entire complexion of the project had changed. António came to us and insisted that we hire Crispy, his uncle, recently returned from a job in Saudi Arabia. Although it was a move we could hardly afford, António was somewhat more than adamant. He wouldn't work with us any longer, he said, unless Crispy was on the job. We didn't like that kind of duress, and it cast a pall over the job site until Paulo and Alberto came forward and apologized for António's behavior. What he had done wasn't right, they said. It was the result of too much alcohol and too little ambition. But Ba was gone and António was coming less and less, so in the end Crispy's wage would not increase our expenses. And Crispy was a good worker, fast and efficient.

We had little choice, really, and so Crispy joined the team. He was a man of about fifty, had a good sense of humor, and did indeed work well until noon. Unfortunately, he drank heavily at lunch, and his work became somewhat wobbly thereafter. So it became a ritual to reassign him in the afternoon to those jobs that required minimal coordination.

And Paulo and Alberto were correct. Once Crispy was installed on the site, António disappeared for an extended period. His mother was visiting from Switzerland, it was rumored. Paulo said that meant António was drinking kirsch.

In António's absence, Paulo and I found that we worked very well together and enjoyed combining our respective skills and backgrounds to resolve complex problems. Paulo even came several times on Saturdays to volunteer his time. He finally realized, he said, that we were truly running out of money and not just making false disclaimers, as was the Portuguese custom.

•

WITHOUT OUR KNOWLEDGE CONSTANCE HAD CONTINUED TO administer Valium to poor Pilote, who passed his days wailing in a corner of China's yard and his nights baying at the moon. Constance's final act of mercy was to free Pilote from his shackles, but due to either his intoxication or his prolonged confinement, he chose not to exercise his rights as a free dog. Unchained, he merely lay down in his usual spot and went to sleep. Undeterred, Constance carried poor Pilote away from the village and deposited him in a lemon orchard.

As Portuguese fate would have it, the next morning Pilote was sighted by the very postman he had bitten several years before. When word filtered back to the village that Pilote had been apprehended and was in the pound, Barbara and I knew it was time to do something. Along with the owners, we went to the Guarda; after lengthy negotiations, we managed to spring the dog from his confinement. The Guarda were glad to see him go, they said. All he did was howl.

That part of the problem resolved, we drove to the beach and confronted Constance, who broke into tears and admitted her culpability. Pilote, she said, was a metaphor for her current existence. Her freedom had become somehow linked with the dog's. A few hours later we were at the airport, our metaphor for "good-bye." We waved Constance off to whatever fate awaited her. We were not unhappy to see her go.

What followed were a few blissful days of dull routine. Paulo and I finished the roof while Alberto, continuing to use the trial-and-error method of electrical engineering, set off loud pops and sparks as he cross-wired everything in sight. Even though he was only semi-competent as an electrician and plumber, he had pulled off a major coup with the telephone company. Proclaiming he had a cousin in Lisbon who worked for the company, he managed to move our application for installation several rungs up the bureaucratic ladder. Now, Alberto contended, it would be only a matter of weeks rather than the two to three years required for most applications. We would have to keep an eye out for the linemen, however, he said. They would come next. And if the right pressure were brought to bear, the right enticement—Alberto lifted an imaginary glass to his lips—they would quickly accommodate us.

As it happened, the linemen appeared on the one day Alberto was absent. Since water was not yet "flowing copiously" as the mayor had promised, we had decided to install two large tanks in the garden, which in combination with a small pump would provide water to the cottage. Poncho, the architect and denizen of the bizarre blue cottage on the main road, had kindly offered to allow us to fill the tanks with water from his private well. But just as we were making the final connection, we saw the linemen approaching and realized we had to act. Alberto had gone off to buy the pump and required fittings, and wouldn't return for several hours. After conferring with Paulo, we decided that I should initiate the attempt at bribery and let Alberto take over when he returned.

Still new to this game, I was somewhat nervous but reckoned the need for a telephone was more important than any ethical considerations, so I ambled down to where the linemen were working and observed for a few moments. There was a whole flock of them, eleven to twelve men, all in different-colored jumpsuits, running around carrying ladders and large spools of cable. I finally selected the one I assumed was the foreman and approached him.

I greeted him, welcomed him to the village, and began to discuss the weather. There wasn't much to be said because the weather was nearly always perfect, but I couldn't find a good hinge in the conversation to open it up to flagrant bribery. Finally, because I could think of nothing else to say, I invited the man down to the bar, indicating that I had several questions I wanted to ask him about Portuguese telecommunications. He looked genuinely surprised for a moment, probably because telecommunications here had hardly evolved beyond two cans and a string. But after considering it for a moment, he called a halt to the work in progress and announced that we were all going to the bar.

José had never seen such a crowd, and not a coffee drinker among them! The workers all took seats, ordered drinks, and began watching television. José gave me an inquiring look from behind his counter, and I indicated grudgingly that I was paying.

I began asking silly questions, hoping that they would somehow culminate in the foreman's ordering the installation of our feeder line that very afternoon. But things did not proceed in such an orderly fashion. Each one of my questions led to

long digressions into obscure technical data. Meanwhile, I noticed that some of the workers had gulped down their first
round and were ordering seconds or thirds. But there was no
derailing the foreman once he got started and had some liquor
in his system. After an hour I thought it best to excuse myself
and leave. That would defuse the situation, I hoped, and give the
linemen a reason to go back to work. So I left the bar, wincing
as I saw the line forming for more refills.

Alberto returned an hour later, and I told him what had
happened. He said that was perfect. I had acted correctly. A few
more words of encouragement, and it would be bad manners
not to install our line. Feeling somewhat relieved, we set off to
find the crew, but we found only their spools and tools exactly
where they had left them, littering the cobbled road. Their
whereabouts was not difficult to discover. There were shouts
and yells coming from the bar. Alberto asked me how long they
had been there.

"Two to three hours now, I think," I replied.

Alberto shook his head. "Not good."

We entered the bar to a scene of general debauchery.
There were glasses everywhere, several people asleep in their
chairs, even a poker game going on at one table. The television
blared with a soccer match, and a couple of workmen were attempting to imitate the intricate footwork of the soccer players
while seated at the dilapidated tables.

"Uh-oh," Alberto groaned, surveying the situation. I noticed that José also seemed to be inebriated.

"This is a big problem," Alberto said.

I agreed.

"No, you don't understand," he said. "These are the wrong
guys."

"What?" I exclaimed.

"These aren't the local guys we need to talk to," Alberto
said. "These guys are from Lisbon. They must be installing new
cable on the main lines. I don't know these guys at all!"

Just as I felt a rush of tears coming to my eyes, the foreman stood and proposed a toast to my generosity. It was all I could do to acknowledge it.

"What are we going to do?" I asked Alberto.

"I don't know, but something quick," Alberto responded. "Remember what happened with the dump truck and the chapel? Well, these guys are more drunk and have even bigger trucks."

Alberto stood thinking for a moment, then left the bar and disappeared down the cobblestoned pathway. I wanted to ask him where he was going, but he was gone before I could formulate the question. An instant later there was a loud snap in the bar, and the lights went out, plunging the dingy little hole into darkness.

Alberto appeared a moment later wiping his hands. He patted me on the back. "As you know I'm very good at creating short circuits," he said.

Certainly true, I thought, watching the drunken linemen stagger to their feet and try to find their way out of the bar.

"Bar is closed. Electrical problem," Alberto kept repeating.

The linemen went out in single file, shading their eyes against the afternoon sun. And with them went José, holding a large soccer scoresheet in his hand. He gave it to me with an apology.

I looked at the piece of paper. Even though his marks were virtually illegible toward the end of the tally sheet, it was obviously a hefty tab.

"Two hundred drinks!" I exclaimed after I counted them up.

"There were even more," José said, diverting his eyes, "but you're a good customer, so I decided to give you a flat rate."

I folded up the slip and put it in my pocket. As for mastering the art of the bribe, maybe one day I would get the hang of it.

Shepherd

28 THE NEXT FEW WEEKS

went by quickly. Spring turned to summer, everyone's mood improved, and the beaches were packed almost every day. The seaside, for the Portuguese, was like an altar that drew huge flocks of worshipers from miles around. Cars jammed with family members, umbrellas, and picnic baskets seemed to form a continuous snake of traffic, winding its way from Lisbon out to the coast. The beach business was in full swing, and whatever couldn't be packed into the trunk of a car could certainly be rented here. Chairs, parasols, water wings, tents—all were available in a multitude of colors for a price. I supposed that even less work than usual was being done in municipal offices.

Barbara and I had little time to relax. Our tenure at Mummy's had already elapsed by two weeks. We had awaited her arrival apprehensively, afraid she would descend on us and throw us out on the street. But in the end only a short letter arrived, saying that she was aware our project was behind schedule. This was Portugal, she said, a place where the word "schedule" really had little meaning. But could we please be out by mid-July? She had several important bridge games planned at the apartment.

Since that didn't really seem feasible, we spent some time looking for other accommodations. But it was high season everywhere, and the very same entrepreneurs who had begged us to do business with them in the winter now turned up their noses. Everything was full, rented, or reserved. "Come back in October," they said, dismissing us offhandedly.

And so we made our decision. We would move into the upper floor of the cottage while we finished the bottom floor. It would be dusty and uncomfortable, but there was really no alternative. We began preparations, and as if the gods approved our decision, we found a tiny kitten abandoned in a plastic bag in the side yard that morning. It was only appropriate to take a kitten along with us to the "House of the Little Cats." So Silas de Várzea, as we called her, was officially adopted and became our mascot. Little did we realize then that she would take the title of the house literally and, although healthy, never grow beyond kitten size.

The one absolute drawback to our plan was, of course, water. Predictably, we had heard nothing from either the mayor or the water company. We had attempted, two weeks previously, what we had hoped would be an official "sit-in" at the water company's headquarters. Barbara and I went to the building and declared that we didn't intend to leave without having a firm commitment to the villagers to begin work on the new water system. We sat for several hours, watching the receptionist knit, then finally asked her if she had forwarded our message.

No, she responded. We hadn't asked her to.

One delay led to another, and eventually everyone left the building, turning off the lights as they went. Sitting in the dark, I commented to Barbara that this wasn't at all how I remembered the sixties. Sit-ins then had been more effective.

Barbara expressed her opinion that for a sit-in to be effective, your adversaries had to understand what a sit-in was. But since nobody seemed to care if we slept in the building, maybe we should move here from Mummy's. "I'm sure at least they have water," she added laconically.

So we made another appointment, this time with the director of the water company, Conception's boss, a man whose very existence was unknown to us until Paulo's relative in the company suggested we meet with him. And we had a new strategy this time. We lined up the biggest, meanest women in the village to accompany us. We figured that their sheer bulk would help get our point across.

On the appointed day we rounded up the women and stuffed them into the Volkswagen van. I checked the springs and shocks to make sure they weren't overloaded, and we headed for Sintra. Barbara and I drilled the women along the way. Although they sounded quite garrulous and tough in the car, we were afraid they would fall silent when confronted with authority figures.

We arrived at the water company and parked, and our entourage threaded through the standard gridlock of people in line. At the guard station—"Checkpoint Charlie," we had begun to call it—we were told it was now required that we wear I.D. badges while inside the building. So we carefully pinned the green laminated cards on one another and proceeded up the staircase. We announced ourselves to the secretary and took seats. Barbara and I sat in the same chairs we had occupied during our abortive attempt at a sit-in.

We were called only a few minutes later and ushered into a large conference room. There was a long, modern, wooden table in the center of the room, and at the far end of the table sat a tall, middle-aged man who was rummaging through a huge mass of paper. He was decidedly un-Portuguese looking—the mayor's cousin, perhaps? He motioned for us to be seated without looking up from the papers. I pulled up chairs for the ladies, arranging them as strategically as possible. A minute later he finished, rubbed his eyes, and addressed us.

"*Bom dia,*" he said and introduced himself as *Senhor* Soares, stating his title and degrees, which were the lengthiest I had yet heard. The village women drew back and dropped their eyes under his barrage of impressive credentials.

It wouldn't do to have the women abashed by authority at such an early stage in the negotiations. So when it was time for me to introduce myself, I took a deep breath and filled the room with a long list of fantasy titles, diplomas, club memberships, and awards. I wasn't really sure where all the words came from. I had never been in a Scottish Rites Temple, nor did I even know the basic precepts of the Rosicrucians. That simple fact, however, did not impede me from proclaiming myself a grand potentate of both as well as several other organizations I made up out of thin air.

It had the desired effect. The village women began to elbow each other and smile. *Senhor* Soares also seemed impressed. Obviously he had never heard of any of the organizations I mentioned. He stood up, shook my hand, and asked what he could do for us.

I explained the situation carefully, including detailed descriptions of our dozen meetings with Conception. Each time I made a particularly salient point, I looked to the women for verbal confirmation. With Barbara's coaxing, they were beginning to warm up slightly now and voiced their approval of my words.

When we had finished presenting our case, Soares thumped the table with his fist and said this was intolerable. He had no knowledge of the situation. A village without water only 18 kilometers from Lisbon? And Portugal on the verge of joining the European Community? Not possible. He would see what was going on. He picked up the phone on the conference table and commanded Conception to appear immediately. Then, reconsidering, he called for all the engineers to come in.

Within five minutes the room was packed with chain-smokers and nail-filers, all of them carrying little dockets in their hands. Soares called the room to order. Then, singling out Conception, he asked her if she was aware of the situation in the village.

Glaring at Barbara and me, she said yes, she was aware, and was currently working on a remedy.

"What remedy?" Soares demanded.

"Well," she began hesitantly, "we had thought of putting a larger water tank at the top of the village."

"Except that a mountain and trees are in the way," I interrupted. Lying through my teeth, I said that when I had performed a certain hydraulic project for the World Health Organization in China, I had required topographical surveys of all the areas involved before formulating any project plans.

"Quite right! Why didn't you do topographical studies?" Soares snapped at Conception.

Conception fiddled nervously with her gold necklace. "I sent a couple of people out."

Soares waved away her response. "Fine, fine, fine," he said. "But what are we doing now?"

Conception looked at the other engineers surrounding her. They held a brief mini-conference in whispers, then Conception said, "We were planning on linking into the main Colares feeder."

I glanced at Barbara. That was certainly news to us.

"And why hasn't this been accomplished?" Soares asked.

Conception again looked around for support. Someone stepped forward and whispered into her ear. I studied all their faces, wondering which one was Paulo's cousin and our mole.

"Well," Conception began again, "it seems the highway commission has refused permission to dig up the road to place the new line."

Soares tapped his pen on the table. "Can they do that?"

"I don't know," Conception said, "but they did."

At that point I took the opportunity to make a new demand. I said I hoped the new water delivery plan also included a plan for sewage disposal. I cited a fictitious project I had worked on recently in Bhutan at the rajah's request where water lines had been run to a village with no combined facilities for waste disposal. The people there, once they had piped water in their homes, immediately began to use it, which caused their primitive septic tanks to flood and rupture. Concluding my remarks, I turned to the village women and gave them the sign. They needed little encouragement now, sensing they had the bureaucrats on the run.

Amelia, our next-door neighbor, spoke first. "That's right," she said. "We want sewers, too!" Inspired by her outburst, the others began to pound on the table, demanding an end to their misery.

Soares finally held up his hand to quiet the commotion. "I will take care of this," he said. "Put in an order for this project to be done immediately," he told Conception. "If the highway commission doesn't like it, that's too bad. Tell them we are required to do it by law."

Then he stood up and addressed our group. "I want to thank you for bringing this matter to our attention," he said to me and shook my hand, "and, of course, for sharing some of your professional experiences with us. Thank you also, ladies."

We left the building in triumph, and Barbara and I took the village women to a café to celebrate with tea and cakes.

Fishmonger

29

A FEW WEEKS LATER WE RE-luctantly moved into Little Cats. We had been left with no other choice. Mummy and her bridge group were bearing down on us momentarily, and the rent, as modest as it was, was becoming more and more of a burden. So we packed our few possessions and, along with the little kitten, made the transfer.

We had found a bedroom set—mahogany and baroque in

design—the previous week in a decrepit bungalow in Azoia, a small coastal village. It consisted of a bedstead and a matching bedside table and chest, all of which fit nicely into the master bedroom with its whitewashed walls and high, dark-stained ceiling.

After a trek to a local *feira,* a flea market, we also collected assorted other essentials, making it possible to live in the cottage in at least a rudimentary fashion. We purchased spoons, forks, knives, pots, pans, sheets, dinnerware, and towels. We bargained perfunctorily for each item, not wanting to lose face and behave like other silly foreigners who paid the asking price, and then moved on. We took everything back to the village in the van and carted it down to the cottage in the original "runaway" wheelbarrow.

Last but not least, we purchased a stereo and color television set with a small cache of money we had previously set aside for just that purpose. They were our small reward for working so hard. We carefully set everything up on the upper floor, then covered it all with sheets of plastic to protect it from the dust that would be created while we finished work on the floor below. We had resigned ourselves to a gritty, dirty existence for a few weeks. Nevertheless, it felt good to be in the cottage surrounded by the fruits of our labors.

Our designs had all worked out very well. The ground-floor arch was finished and the spiral staircase, scrubbed and painted, was in place. Paulo had plastered the fireplace while I finished the chimney up on the roof. António's wine rack was superb, although he constantly moaned about the fact that we hadn't yet filled it up. My rustic kitchen cabinets had been installed, and all that was missing from the ground floor now were the stone pavers and a kitchen sink.

The upper floor was complete. The "queen's" bathtub was the highlight of the new bathroom, surrounded by a panel of white and blue *azulejo* tiles. Alberto had artfully placed a porcelain sink—discovered in the debris on the ground floor—into a shallow niche that Paulo had sculpted in the wall. Alberto had also managed to place an array of electric outlets throughout the cottage but had not yet identified each circuit among the jumble of wires that converged at the new, bright blue fuse box. He seemed to prefer the far less dangerous task of running extensions for the telephone line that had finally arrived.

The pump perched on the water tanks in the garden now provided us with water, fed through an intricate maze of copper pipes and warmed by a small gas heater that Alberto had successfully installed after only two minor explosions. We had also plumbed the kitchen and bathroom, and built a new, larger septic tank to replace the inadequate cesspool in the garden. In a crude fashion we now had almost all the comforts of home. I had even hooked up the gas stove temporarily on the upper floor next to the refrigerator, both of which awaited their place in the kitchen still under construction. But without a sink for washing dishes we ate out often and had morning coffee at the bar. We spoke little or not at all about the fact that we would soon have to put our beautiful little cottage on the market.

The morning after we moved in, Paulo and I were laying the ancient flagstones again for the kitchen floor when we made a discovery: During the act of scooping out soil to form a firm base for the giant stones, we hit on something solid. We carefully dug the object out of the undisturbed earth and brushed it off. It was a smooth stone hammer head, obviously very old.

Paulo held it up. "At least three hundred years old," he said.

Crispy had a look at it, turning it over in his hand slowly. "More like four hundred years, I think," he said. "We used to find them in the desert in Saudi."

Alberto appeared, scrutinized the ancient piece of stone, and whistled. "This belongs in the Sintra museum. It's two thousand years old if a day."

Our conversation was interrupted by the noise of an approaching motorbike, and we all stopped to listen. It certainly sounded like António's mufflerless piece of scrap metal. He hadn't come to work in over two weeks, but it was indeed António, looking very dapper in clean pants and a short-sleeved shirt. He wasn't here to work by any chance, I asked him.

No, no, he replied. He couldn't work right now. His mother was visiting from Switzerland, and, well, he had to look after her.

I said I was sorry. I didn't know she wasn't well.

António laughed, and the crew along with him. "It's not that at all," he said. "I have to protect her from the men."

"*Ela é uma beleza da primeira!*" Paulo chipped in.

"António's mother a beauty?" I asked jokingly. "Does she have a neck?"

"*E mais!*" Alberto exclaimed. "And more!"

António slapped me on the shoulder in jest, and sent me halfway across the yard.

"So," I said. "This is just a social visit?"

No, António said. He had something else in mind. But by the way, it was getting near the end of the project, and he wanted to see if I was able to lift the cement mixer yet.

Huh, I responded. There was little time to play with the thing. I rarely touched it, I said, indulging in a blatant lie.

Not to worry, António said. That wasn't really the reason he was here. No. He was here because today was the day of the meal—the lunch that he and the others owed us as a result of our bet about the fireplace. We did want to collect, didn't we?

"Yes, definitely," I said.

"Good then," António said. "Noon at the bar."

At exactly noon, we all set down our tools and washed our hands and even our faces. Nothing less would do at what promised to be a unique event. As far as we knew, the bar had never served a meal before. The only food available there was stale crackers and small packets of chewing gum. We had no idea what Maria, José's wife, might be cooking up. Or was it going to be catered?

Paulo, Alberto, and Crispy were excited, too. A special lunch meant lingering over coffee and *aguardente,* talking about soccer, and in general whiling away the afternoon hours in idle pursuits rather than plastering or laying stone. Barbara and I had also decided to give up for the day. After the meal we would go for a walk in the forest and take pictures of the cottage from a distance, pictures that we would inevitably have to send to real estate agents.

As we approached the bar, we noticed it looked different. Someone had swept the front stoop and even put down a ragged rubber doormat. We wiped our feet carefully and peered into the dim recesses of the little dive we had become so fond of. It was ominously quiet for the noon hour, and as our eyes adjusted to the dim light, we realized that no one was there. The usual number of stray dogs was curled up in the corners, but all the rickety tables had been pushed aside with the exception of one large table that was now covered with a plastic red-and-white-checkered tablecloth. On the table were napkins, silverware, salt and pepper shakers—even a candle. We were very impressed.

José suddenly appeared from the doorway beyond which we knew he and his wife had a bedroom next to the kitchen. He wore a fresh white shirt and a little bow tie. There was a white napkin draped over his arm. He shook our hands and pulled out the chairs for us, brushing imaginary dust from the seats. We were going to eat very well, he said. Very well, indeed. Maria had been a cook in a restaurant in Lisbon once and knew the culinary arts.

José poured us glasses of white wine with a flourish, and as we toasted the village, each other, and then Portugal in general, *Dona* China appeared in the doorway, pushing herself along with her cane.

"*Está fechado hoje!*" José barked at her.

"Closed?" she responded. "What do you mean, closed? The door is open, and I have to see 'Rain in the Sand' on television this afternoon."

"Special party today," José said, warning her away.

China peered at us through the doorway. "Ah, my neighbors!" she said. "It's you! You're having a party, and you didn't invite me? *Po, po, po.*"

I was embarrassed and told her that actually António had arranged the party as payment for a bet we had made.

"I see," China said. "But you won't mind if I sit in the corner over here and watch, will you? I haven't been to a party in years, and who knows? If the good God is in your heart today, you might even throw me a scrap for lunch, eh?"

José again said that the bar was closed, but China just sat herself down in the doorway. "Don't worry about me," she said. "I'll be good. And I'll keep others from bothering us if they try to get in." She waved her cane in the air.

I told José that was fine with us and asked him to give her a glass of wine.

António finally arrived and joined us, filling up half the table with his girth. He had a mischievous twinkle in his eye. "You're going to eat something you've never had before," he said, "a real Portuguese delicacy. Not like those things you fix."

He was referring to the peanut butter and jelly sandwiches Barbara and I often packed for lunch. We had given him one once. He spit it out and said it tasted like paste. It had taken him three days of serious drinking to get the taste out of his mouth, he declared—three days that he didn't come to work, of course.

A couple of villagers appeared at the door of the bar, but China chased them away with the tip of her cane. "Special party here!" she barked at them. "Go get drunk somewhere else!"

José emerged from the kitchen with a steaming tureen of soup and went around the table ladling out copious amounts into our hefty ceramic bowls. It was a standard *caldo verde,* or vegetable soup, but very good. We ate in silence and apprehension as we wondered what the main course might be. Barbara was fidgeting in her chair, trying to peek into the kitchen to see what might be coming next.

"Is it good?" China inquired.

"Very good," Barbara replied.

"I wouldn't know. I never eat fresh food," China said. "I just eat what comes in cans or what the dog leaves me. Pilote's better now, you know. He doesn't sound like Elvis Presley anymore."

Barbara and I exchanged guilty looks. Then Barbara asked José to bring China some soup, which she declined. "Good food might upset my stomach," she said. "But I only have a few days left on the planet anyway, so I guess I'll eat it."

A few minutes later our soup bowls were whisked away, glasses exchanged, and a red wine served. I sniffed the air to see if there were any telltale odors that might give away the nature of the main event.

China finished her soup and thanked us, raising her wineglass. "This is good wine," she said. "But be careful! Don't drink too much. I've had a problem with this wine lately. It makes me think the walls in my bedroom are moving."

"Oh, really?" Barbara said in her most innocent voice.

"One of them moves a lot and changes color, too."

Paulo was kicking me under the table.

"But I'm old," China sighed. "And senile and stupid and ugly. I would be a witch, but I can't afford a broom."

Several more people arrived at the bar's entrance, only to be repelled by China's cane. But when she told them it was a private party, they formed a little half-circle just beyond the doorway, peering in to try to see what was going on.

Just then José entered from the kitchen and clapped his hands together for attention. *"Mesdames et messieurs,"* he said, bowing at the waist. He directed our attention to Maria who came out of the kitchen carrying a huge steaming platter in both hands. She set it down on the table with great pride.

The quartet of masons announced their delight in unison.

"Caras de bacalhau!"

And that was just what it was—a platter of fish heads.

Cod heads, to be exact. Dozens of steaming fish heads complete with glazed-over eyes.

Barbara turned white, and I tried to smile. Outside the bar, the growing crowd of people clapped when they saw the heaping platter arrive.

Alberto must have noticed our dismay. "You don't like this?" he asked.

"Well, I don't know," I said. "We've never had fish heads before."

"It's a great thing," Alberto declared. "A national delicacy. And very expensive!"

"They look wonderful," I said, taking a huge gulp of red wine.

António served Barbara a large portion of heads, piling them high on her plate over her protests. China had even risen from her seat by the doorway and approached to inspect the delicacy. "They look good," she said. "I had them once fifty years ago on my honeymoon. They make you very strong in bed!"

I thanked her for her wisdom and gave her my plate, which Alberto had filled with the loathsome food. Unfortunately, he quickly served me another.

"Let me show you how you eat them," he said and began a graphic demonstration of how to extricate the jowl meat from around the little teeth. When he showed us how to pop the eyes out, I saw that Barbara was about to faint. I got up quickly, went to her side of the table, and fanned her face with a napkin.

"Too much excitement," I said to the masons. "Too much heat." At the same time, under my breath, I whispered to Barbara, "The dogs. The dogs."

Attracted by the smell of the food, the stray dogs were sitting under and around the table, and Barbara got the message. She speared a fish head on her plate, raised it to her mouth, then dropped it to the napkin on her lap when no one was looking. From there it took only a small flick of her hand to brush the fish head onto the floor where the dogs took care of the rest. I decided to use a different technique and managed to swallow a few of the greasy little tidbits with copious mouthfuls of red wine. I had to work quickly. I would be very drunk in a few minutes.

But the room was filled with noise and hearty laughter, and I realized that the joy we had come to know here in the village stemmed from situations exactly like this. It was the anticipation of the unexpected that kept our lives so full and intriguing. And when it happened, we could never know just what to expect next. António might come to work, or he might not; Alberto might continue to crosswire the electrical circuits, or he might finally set it right; the village might have water someday, but then again it might not.

It was a gentle and benign form of chaos, and only a madman would dare to dream of order and perfection. But in this sunny village no one seemed bothered by uncertainty. Indeed, in some way they seemed to relish it, for in the end it brought us all together.

Whitewashing the Cottage

30

TWO WEEKS LATER OUR renovation project was completed. "Completed" was, of course, a totally inaccurate word to describe it. There were still many things to be done, but they were jobs Barbara and I could handle alone—more or less.

It was a very sad afternoon when we had to say good-bye to the masons. They had become family, and we would miss them each in a different way. It was hard to imagine lunchtime without Alberto roasting ribs or chicken over a fire in the little garden. Or Paulo with his birdlike voice shouting for António to buckle up his drooping pants. And what would our days be like without António's generous smile and his creative excuses for avoiding work and enjoying life?

There were tears in our eyes as we watched them pack up their tools carefully in leather pouches. But we knew we would see them often. In fact, our recommendations had landed them another renovation job. Nevertheless, their departure signaled the end of a unique time in our lives. Even though we thought the renovation had dragged on forever, we had finished it in relatively record time. And now we lived in the House of the Little Cats with our kitten. We had accomplished what everyone told us could never be done.

A truck finally arrived to cart off the concrete-form lumber, the scaffolding, and the large barrels we had used for water storage. It was then that António came to me with the chain saw in his hand.

"What are we going to do about this?" he asked.

"What do you mean?" I responded, feigning ignorance.

"Our agreement. Lift the cement mixer, or I get to keep the chain saw. Remember?"

Of course I remembered. And even though I had tried every morning when no one was about, I never got the enormous thing off the ground. But I wasn't about to give up. To see António lift it, at least I had to make an effort.

I looked António dead in the eye. "Stand back," I said.

He smiled his huge smile and whistled. Then he called everyone to come and watch. Within minutes a large crowd had gathered, not exactly the forum I had hoped for but there was no turning back now.

Paulo pulled me aside. "Don't do it," he warned. "You'll kill yourself and ruin your back."

I tried to wink at him to allay his fears, but it turned out to be more of a flutter. I approached the monstrous machine and noticed that it was totally clean for its trip to its next temporary home. That would subtract a few kilos, I thought.

I stretched for a moment, then stood up against the machine and grasped the two bars on either side of the bucket. For some strange reason I focused on the stone dolmenlike structures that peppered the Sintra range. I took a deep breath of pine-scented mountain air, closed my eyes, and began to tug at the bars, every muscle straining. Voices shouted encouragement as I tried to lift the machine. My head buzzed, and I broke into a sweat. Then suddenly there was cheering.

Opening my eyes, I looked down to see the cement mixer a full two inches off the ground. I was so surprised, I dropped it and fell over backward. Barbara and Paulo helped me up as everyone clapped—everyone except António. He was shaking his head.

"Not bad for a foreigner," he said, patting me on the back. "But you didn't understand the rules."

"What do you mean?"

António walked over to the mixer, knelt down with his back to it, reached over his shoulder with one hand, and grasped the center pinion of the mixer bucket. He shouted once and stood up slowly, lifting the mixer with one hand over his head. He set it back down again on the back of the truck, then picked up the chain saw and placed it in the truck next to the mixer.

"I guess I forgot to mention," he said, "that you had to lift it with one hand."

He waved and climbed on the back of the truck. The others followed after we had embraced fondly. And all I could do was laugh as the truck pulled away. António was living proof that if you wanted something in Portugal, you could not hope to get it in any reasonable way. For here there were no rational expectations, only improvisations. And there were no rules, absolutely no rules. You simply made them up as you went along through life.

Village Wild Life

31

A FEW DAYS LATER, RE-
morsefully, we put the House of the Little Cats on the market.
We called all the listed agents, even Sara, and announced our intention. No one seemed at all excited by the house's prospects,
and very few agents even showed up to have a look. Those who
did dwelled on the obvious imperfections: The house did not
permit access by car; there were too many chickens running

around or too many dogs, not to mention that the neighbor's yard smelled of excrement. The village itself was also in sad shape, they said as they shook their communal heads and declared the cottage impossible to sell. People want modern things, not old oddities with windows that don't match and huge thick walls. No, no, it would never sell at any price.

We were somewhat discouraged but determined to show them otherwise. We knew the cottage would not appeal to Portuguese sensibilities, so we decided to advertise it ourselves in the *Anglo-Portuguese News,* a journal for expatriates that came out weekly. It proved to be a big mistake. We received a multitude of calls in various languages and were in turn visited by the world's greatest assortment of eccentrics and maniacs. It was summer, it seemed, and touring houses for sale was a simple, economical way to pass those idle days of vacation when they weren't lying on the beach.

Groups both large and small arrived unannounced, knocking on our door and demanding to see our handiwork. Since they had no intention of buying, they were intensely critical, and we almost always ended up defending our every design decision. With Sandra's help we finally put a sign on the door—SHOWN BY APPOINTMENT ONLY—in six different languages. That seemed to deter no one, however. Rather than call the number printed on the sign, they would pound on the door until we answered and say they had little time before their flight back to Lyon or Frankfurt. They must see the house now.

We accommodated as many as we could, still trying to finish the painting of the exterior and complete the kitchen. But we quickly came to realize that our love of the village and its inhabitants could not be communicated successfully during a single rapid visit. Their innate gentility and mild manners were always eclipsed by the shoddy state of their houses, dogs, and roads. So, logically enough, we took it upon ourselves to upgrade the village's entire image.

We chose the path that prospective buyers would have to follow to reach the cottage. Then we approached the villagers who lived along the way and offered to whitewash their facades or replaster their crumbling walls. It was basic low-tech stuff that we could accomplish easily enough with materials left over from Little Cats. But much to our dismay, we found our neighbors very reluctant. For us to offer to repair their houses seemed to force them to admit that something was amiss in their world. Their initial response was always suspicion and denial. As we talked further and tried to convince them of our good intentions, they generally relaxed and in the end agreed with our assessment of what needed to be done. But, they all said, we need not do it. They themselves would carry out the plastering and painting. We had done enough for the village, they said. We had approached the water company on their behalf, and although nothing had yet come of that, they were very appreciative of our efforts. We had worked hard on our own house and should now rest and enjoy the fruits of our labors.

We agreed and wished we could do just that. But reality wore a different face, and already we were into our last cash reserves. We would have to pursue another plan. And so we did what we could for urban renewal. We swept the streets and picked up loose garbage. At night we mended fences and put what chickens we could catch back in their yards. Then when we received a call that someone was coming to look at Little Cats, we swung into action. Barbara would go down to the local butcher, from whom we had purchased the rock-hard beef. There she would obtain more of the same meat which she would use to lure the stray packs of dogs off into the forest. Due to the meat's elasticity and obstinacy, devouring it took hours and ensured that the meanest of the "mangies" would not be around to bite prospective buyers. I, in turn, would go down to the main road, pick up all the garbage from the overflowing trash cans, and bag it, hoping to create the illusion of tidiness and order.

Then together we would quickly sweep the cobblestones and take our neighbor's laundry off the line so that it would not obstruct the view to the sea directly in front of the cottage.

We felt like designers creating the set for a movie being filmed in a quaint Portuguese village. But poverty and the less than enthusiastic remarks of the real estate agents convinced us that we had to make an extra effort if we were to get buyers beyond their first impressions. Still a dozen or so buyers continued to turn up their noses, and our plan didn't seem to be paying off.

Then on a warm Sunday morning we received another call and went into action again. Two English ladies were coming to view the cottage. Barbara, who had spent several years in England, certified their accent as definitely upper class. She ran off to the butcher's shop to beg scraps while I rounded up a few chickens and hid João's rusty motorbike in China's yard next to Pilote. I filled a basket with lemons from our lemon trees and placed it on the wall in front of the house as a prop. I would pick it up later so it would appear that I was just coming in from the orchard with the day's bounty. Barbara, after leading the dogs into the forest, went down to wait on the lower road to make sure that the ladies did not stray from our prearranged route. A noisy group of village boys was playing soccer in the middle of the road, but I dispatched them with a few candy bars and a promise to referee their game later on in the day.

The ladies finally arrived in full designer attire. Barbara led them down the path to the cottage, and I appeared to greet them carrying the basket of lemons. I was just coming from the garden right over there, I said. Yes, it goes with the house, and there's a lovely nêspera tree that produces enough fruit to pay for the house in two years. We had learned our parts in this comedy well.

The ladies looked around, had tea, and looked some more. They loved the house and the view of the sea. They loved its historic continuity as evidenced by the ancient stone hammer head we had found, now displayed on the fireplace mantle. And they loved the climate. The village, well, it was quaint, wasn't it?

The ladies asked to see the garden and the view again. Tall and regal, they went outside while Barbara and I stayed behind, knowing intuitively that this was the moment of decision. There was nothing more we could do or say. The House of the Little Cats, the garden, the view, even the village must now speak for themselves. We watched them circling the garden, talking quietly.

When they returned to the house, they had made up their minds. They shook our hands and said, yes, they would buy the cottage for the price we were asking. They had only to speak to one of their husbands, a barrister, to arrange the paperwork and monetary transfer. Unfortunately, they could not give us a deposit now because they were going directly to the airport and had no cash. Nor could they write us a check. But we were American and they were English, we spoke the same language. There wouldn't be any problems, they were sure. They would send money directly upon their return to London.

We walked them down the prescribed pathway to their rental car, hoping that the dogs, chickens, and rowdy boys were not waiting in ambush. We waved good-bye as they drove off, and once they were out of sight, Barbara and I embraced with tears in our eyes. We would be able to eat now, but it was still difficult to think of leaving the House of the Little Cats. It was the first house we had ever owned together, and we had worked so hard on it. The crew—Paulo, Alberto, even António—had created certain things especially for us. And what would China do without us? Would the English ladies give her food?

•

A FEW DAYS LATER WE WENT TO LISBON TO CELEBRATE. WE employed our favorite tactic, which was to go to an early movie matinee somewhere in the city center. Then, just as it was closing and almost empty, we stopped by the Gulbenkian Museum to look at the fine collection of ancient art and Lalique jewelry.

After that we strolled through the museum's gardens, fragrant with acanthus and jasmine, and took the metro back downtown. A short but tough climb up the steep Rua da Gloriana, and we were in the Bairro Alto, ready for dinner. There were hundreds of restaurants to choose from, each with a different decor and cuisine. We walked down the narrow, busy streets and examined the posted menus until we found something intriguing. After dinner we walked back down to Rossio station, guided by ancient streetlights. There we boarded the antiquated train for Sintra, where our trusty blue van awaited us. We drove home to the village under bright starlight and past sleeping manor houses.

That night, however, our return to the House of the Little Cats was somewhat different. An eerie light rain had begun falling, and the shadows of the village seemed somehow diffused, distorted. We parked the van and began to walk toward the cottage. As we rounded the last corner of the cobblestoned path, we saw that the main gate of Little Cats was wide open, swinging in the wind. I thought it very strange because I had carefully double-locked it when we had left just a few hours before. Something was wrong, and as if to confirm our fears, our kitten, Silas de Várzea, emerged from the garden, yowling. Panicking now, we entered the garden to find what we had suspected: The house had been robbed. The front gate had been forced with some type of bar and the doors to the kitchen battered with a blunt object until the lock had given way.

Barbara began to cry. The memory of being robbed in Avignon was still too fresh in her mind. I was angry as I walked through the house to determine what had been stolen. We had very few things of value, I realized quickly—only our new stereo system and the color television. I went directly to where they were supposed to be and found only vacant space and dangling antenna wires.

In the bedroom I saw that the mattress had been jostled off the bed, an obvious attempt to see if we had anything hidden underneath. I went out through the bedroom door and down the outer staircase. When I came back into the kitchen, I found Barbara hiding behind the door with a huge bottle in her hand ready to clout me over the head.

"I thought it was them," she said, "coming back to take more."

I told her that the stereo and television were gone, which brought a renewed burst of tears. "Maybe I can catch them down on the road," I said, wanting to do something.

A few minutes later I was driving along the road to Colares when I saw Jacinto, one of the villagers, obviously very intoxicated. I pulled over to the side of the road and questioned him. Had he seen anyone go by in the opposite direction? He finally understood after I repeated the question several times; he answered no.

Someone with a stereo, I said. Someone carrying a television?

Jacinto gave me a very puzzled look and asked, "Why, what's playing?"

I told him briefly that we had just returned from Lisbon to find the house broken into. Even in his alcoholic haze, that seemed to upset Jacinto. He took off his cap and slapped it on his knee. "No one's going to rob *Senhor* Ricardo!" he shouted. "You must go to the Guarda right now!"

I thought that was a good idea and thanked him, refusing his numerous pleas to come with me. Several minutes later I was at the local police station, staring through the glass door at an officer sleeping with his head on the desk. I banged several times on the door until he finally raised his head.

"What is it?" he asked.

I told him we had just been robbed.

"Come back in the morning," he said, dropping his head back down on the desk.

I assumed that he had been at the same bar as Jacinto, but I continued to shout that the robbery had just occurred, probably within the last hour or so. The trail must still be "hot," and we could catch the culprits if only he would wake up and help me.

He did get up, but only to pull the shade down over the window so I couldn't bother him anymore.

I drove through the hills for another twenty minutes or so but found no clues. My anger had cooled somewhat. After all, it was only money. Whoever had stolen the stereo and the television probably didn't want them for resale. No, this area was still poor compared to other districts. Whoever had done it would probably keep them for himself.

Back at Little Cats there was a great commotion. All the lights were on, and I heard loud noises of general hysteria. Fearing for Barbara's safety, I ran into the kitchen and found almost the entire village assembled there. Young and old, men and women alike were all dressed in their nightclothes and holding glasses of wine in their hands. As soon as they saw me enter, a wave of anguish and tears flooded the room. Several people embraced me warmly, apologizing for the great shame that had befallen them and the village. Barbara and Ricardo robbed! It was just not possible, they said. We had done so much for the village and now this! Shame, shame.

Someone handed me a glass of wine. João the Thief's wife handed me a pill. It was a Valium. One of the village boys offered Barbara a puppy from his dog's latest litter. It was a grand party, and under different circumstances we might have enjoyed it. But it was 3:00 A.M. by now, and I wanted to be first in line at the Guarda in the morning. So gradually and as politely as I could, I led our concerned neighbors out into the garden and thanked them for coming to our aid and assistance.

Edmundo, our next-door neighbor, pulled me aside as he left. "You know who did it, don't you?" he asked.

"No," I said. "Who? João?"

Edmundo shook his head. "No, he's still scared of António.

No, it has to be the other one, the one who's been visiting lately. What's his name? Mathias."

I was shocked. Mathias was the young man with drug and alcohol problems whom Barbara had been teaching how to paint in her spare time.

"It couldn't be Mathias," I said. "He's our friend. He's even had dinner with us several times."

Edmundo shrugged. "That's the way it is here," he said. "In Latin countries you steal from your friends."

He walked down the path to his house. I stood and thought for a moment, then suddenly realized he was right.

The next morning at seven o'clock I was at the Guarda's front door just as it was unlocked for the day's business.

"What is the problem?" the attending sergeant asked me.

"Robbery," I said.

He looked surprised. "Oh? When?"

I told him what had happened and when.

He shook his head. "You should have come here right away."

"I did," I said. "The officer on duty was asleep."

He again seemed incredulous. "Here? You came here to this office?"

"Yes, yes," I insisted. "I knocked on this door, and the guard was sleeping with his head on that table."

"Not possible," the sergeant declared. "We are all professionals here. But do not worry, we will get the man. He who works by night sleeps by day."

With these words of wisdom I was ushered into the station. More uniformed men appeared, and I was forced to repeat my story over and over. Finally I suggested that someone write it down so I wouldn't have to repeat it again. My suggestion was greeted warmly, and it was immediately decided that an official report should be made out. I was shown to a desk and surrounded by young guards, all eager to assist in writing the report. But they could not agree about what date to put on it and how to fill it out properly.

After an hour or so of conjecture and argument, the report was complete. I was beginning to get a little bit impatient, convinced as I now was that Mathias was the culprit and that every moment we spent here haggling over punctuation was a moment lost to pursuit. When I pointed this out to the sergeant, he held his hand up solemnly. Nothing could be done, he said, without the approval of Comandante Bernardo, who had not yet arrived. He would be along shortly, he assured me, as soon as his morning drive was finished.

I tried to relax, but it was not easy. I could already picture our stereo and television heading toward Lisbon on the back of a truck. When they brought me coffee, I began to wonder how they had ever apprehended anyone. If law enforcement was akin to all the other bureaucracies I had encountered, the burglars in this area should be prosperous indeed.

Half an hour later a solemn hush fell over the office, and a short, stolid man entered. He was dressed in a clean starched uniform ablaze with colorful decorations. His hat was tucked neatly under an epaulet, and he wore not one but two automatic pistols. It was Comandante Bernardo, who paused and waited while a young guard struck a match and lit the cigarette that he had removed from a solid silver case and put in his mouth. The other officers stood and saluted the great man as he walked past.

The *comandante* disappeared into his office. Assuming that he would see me directly, I attempted to follow him, but the sergeant cut me off. I would have to wait a few minutes, he said. The *comandante* must have his coffee before he began his investigations. So I sat down again and watched as trays of coffee and sweets were delivered from the café across the street to the *comandante*'s office.

Forty-five minutes later I was finally summoned. I was

shown into a dim little cubicle and told to sit across the desk from the *comandante*. He was engaged in reading through a huge sheaf of papers, smoke from his cigarette swirling around his head and drifting up toward the ceiling. One of his underlings stood at attention by his side.

He finally looked up from the papers, grunted, and offered me a cigarette from the silver case that now sat on his desk. I declined politely but not before Bernardo gave me a stare that obviously questioned my manhood. Finally he got up, lit another cigarette, inhaled deeply, and said, *"E então?"*

When I again explained what had happened, Bernardo looked very surprised.

"Robbery? Here? In my jurisdiction?"

Yes, I said.

"Hmmmm." He smoked and paced. "Are you sure that you have not just misplaced the objects?"

I said I was quite sure. Locks had been broken, and the thief was probably getting away as we spoke.

He raised his hand. "Do not worry. Those who work by night sleep by day."

Perhaps so, but it was getting on toward noon, and I wasn't really sure how late those "who worked by night" might sleep into the next day. I was about to say something to that effect when Bernardo asked, "And what exactly do you want me to do?"

I replied that it would be nice if he could catch the thief.

"I see," Bernardo said, still pacing behind his desk. "And do you have an idea who this person might be?"

Yes, I had an idea, but I told him I wasn't one hundred percent sure.

Bernardo took a sip from his coffee and sighed. "Well, if you know who the thief is, why don't you simply go to him and confront him? Ask him to give your things back."

I was not really surprised by his suggestion. I had become accustomed to the rather bizarre permutations of reason that ruled Portuguese bureaucracies. Try as I might, however, I couldn't imagine Barbara and me knocking on Mathias's door and accusing him of robbing us. We would feel very ashamed if we were wrong. And if we were right, what then? But I knew better than to state my reservations to that line of action directly, so I went for an oblique angle. I told Bernardo that we thought the thief might have a gun.

He frowned deeply as he considered that possibility. After pacing a while longer, he opened the top drawer of his desk, pulled out an automatic pistol in a holster, and plopped it down on the desk. "I will lend you my gun in the name of the law."

I stared down at the weapon. It had a pearl-handled grip, and the bullets in the holster looked like silver. But I could not see myself brandishing it in front of Mathias. Again risking my already tenuous manhood, I admitted that I had no idea how to use a gun.

That seemed to exasperate Bernardo. He pounded his fist lightly on the desk several times, then commanded the underling to put the pistol back in the drawer. "Well," he said, looking me directly in the eye, "what do you expect me to do?"

Not wanting to offend him with my obviously biased cultural opinions, I said that in the movies the police always sent a couple of officers to investigate an allegation and take appropriate action.

"A couple of men?" Bernardo exclaimed. "Two of my very busy men?"

I said that two of his less busy men would be fine, but I wondered just what might be keeping all these men so busy if not crimes.

Bernardo looked down at the written report and my signature. A flicker of recognition crossed his face, and he asked if I was the one who was causing such a fuss with the water company. I was? Good, he said. They were a lousy bunch of meddlers, and all the water systems should be put in his hands where they belonged. He would straighten out the mess! He shouted a command, and I heard the men in the outside office scrambling to their feet.

Bernardo led me out of his cubicle into the outer office where his men were standing rigidly at attention. He checked them over carefully, then said to me, "Pick two. They will go with you. They know how to shoot."

I chose two inordinately small guards. Everyone seemed surprised by my selection, and so, quite frankly, was I. But I didn't have time to reconsider. Bernardo barked orders at the two men and dismissed the others. He shook my hand, wished me good luck on my mission, and returned to his office.

Not quite sure how to proceed, I went outside and climbed into the police jeep. A few seconds later my two recruits came out, saw me in the jeep, and froze. I asked them what was the matter, and they responded that I was sitting in the *comandante*'s jeep. It was forbidden to sit in his jeep without being assigned to it.

All right, I said, which vehicle should we go in?

They looked at each other and conversed briefly in a dialect I found hard to understand. Finally they told me there was no other vehicle. We would have to walk. Was it far? they inquired. If so, maybe we should have a coffee and some pastries before we set off.

No, I said, it wasn't far at all. And we would go in my van but hide it before we approached so the suspect would not see it coming and run.

The two men conferred again and announced that this was fine and good but that coffee would render them more alert and courageous.

I told them that speed was of the essence. Otherwise the thief might get away.

They opened their mouths in unison. "Those who work by night—" I cut them off. It was already afternoon, I said, and the thief had had ample time to rest and recuperate and perhaps even plan his next caper.

They gave up and climbed into the back of the van, and we set off for the alleged thief's house. They lit cigarettes, and I could hear them talking about the theft of a chicken in one of their villages and how, through clever police work, the purloined bird had been tracked down and returned to its owner.

I drove around the last corner and pulled the van off the road into a thicket of trees. We all got out, and I pointed to Mathias's house. Yes, yes, they said. They saw it. But for some reason they didn't move.

Were they going up to the house, I asked.

They looked at each other with puzzlement. Well, no, they said. They weren't sure. Bernardo had instructed them only to accompany me. He hadn't told them to "do" anything.

But come on, I said. Someone had to go up to the house. It was really their duty. What would people think if I went up there and got shot?

Like Bernardo, they were suddenly very eager to lend me their pistols, adding, however, that Bernardo had given them no bullets.

Exasperated, I asked them if there had ever been any robberies here before.

They said that they thought there had been a few.

And how did Bernardo deal with those incidents, I asked.

They said that Bernardo had gone to the local café and demanded that the stolen goods be returned or else he would beat the thief.

And what happened?

The goods had been returned immediately, but Bernardo had given the robber a good trashing anyway.

And why didn't Bernardo go to the café in this case?

Simple, they said. That café was currently closed for renovations.

I gave up and decided on action. All right, I told the two men, I would go up to the house alone. But if I got beat up, it would be their responsibility, and with that announcement I strode off toward the house. Stopping halfway I found that the two guards were close behind me.

What were they doing now, I asked.

Protecting me, they said. They didn't want to get in trouble if I got killed or worse.

I told them that it was silly for all of us to go. They should go, I said. I knew the house and would cover the rear entrance in case the thief tried to escape.

They finally agreed, walked to the front door, and knocked. Someone opened the door, but I couldn't see who it was. There was a brief exchange of words, then one of the guards returned to where I was standing.

"What exactly was stolen?" he asked.

I patiently described again what had been stolen. The guard went back up to the door, and suddenly both of them went inside the house.

A full half-hour went by before they reappeared, walking slowly up the road toward me. They looked very solemn.

"Well," I asked. "Any luck?"

They stared down at the road. "Yes," they said in unison. "We found the articles."

I was very excited by the news. They, however, seemed not at all elated.

"That's wonderful," I said. "Where were they?"

"Under the bed," one of them replied.

"And Mathias," I asked. "He wasn't there?"

Yes, they responded. He was there, but he was sleeping.

So they were right, I thought. He was sleeping by day and working by night. Very few things had been so simple in this country.

"So what do we do now?" I asked, assuming that we could just collect the stereo and the television, and I could bring them home.

The smaller of the two men spoke up. "We must call Bernardo. He may want to come and make the arrest."

I was shocked. "Can't you arrest him yourself?"

Impossible, they said. Bernardo made all the arrests. Arresting someone was tantamount to declaring his guilt, and how could they be sure?

I pointed out that in this case the evidence was fairly overwhelming.

Nevertheless, they said, it would not do to proceed without Comandante Bernardo. They must find a phone or, even better, go back to headquarters to report. And with that statement they both got back into the car.

I refused to leave. What would happen if Mathias woke up and ran off with the goods?

They both frowned and shook their heads. That wouldn't happen, they said. They had left a note next to the bed, explaining to Mathias that they had been there and that he should not move or touch anything. They had also told his mother not to let him out of the house.

I still wasn't pleased with the way all this was going. "Maybe one of you should stay here and watch the house," I suggested. "Let the other one go and report to Bernardo."

Not possible, they said. They were trained to work in teams, and a team should never be separated. As a team they were three. As individuals they were only one.

I realized it was futile to discuss yet another of their aphorisms. But then I noticed that a phone line ran from the roof of Mathias's house back up to the road. "There you go," I said. "You can use the phone at the thief's house to call the *comandante*. That way you won't have to worry about him escaping."

They discussed this suggestion in whispers and told me it was highly irregular. But in the end they agreed to do it—if, they said, Mathias's mother agreed to let them back in the house.

So they returned to the house and disappeared inside once again. By now all this activity had drawn a small crowd, and Mathias's father, a farmworker, had come out of the fields and stood a short distance from the house, curious about what was going on.

A few minutes later the two guards came out again, this time carrying our stereo and television. Mathias, looking extremely unkempt, shuffled along closely behind them.

"Bernardo told us to bring it all in and the thief, too," they said when they reached the car. They then proceeded to load the stolen items roughly into the back of the van.

Mathias came to a halt a few paces away from me and diverted his eyes from my stare. But suddenly he advanced and embraced me. "I'm sorry," he said. "Really sorry. I was doing drugs and unaware. I was going to bring the things back to you today."

I felt sincerely sorry for him until I remembered how deliberately the locks had been broken and the wet, arduous path through the forest that he would have been forced to take to avoid being seen. All that couldn't have been accomplished by someone high on drugs.

Mathias lit a cigarette. "I have a favor to ask," he said. "Can we wait until my father returns to the fields before we go to the station? Otherwise he will be angry. The shame." His voice trailed off as he inhaled.

I was weakening emotionally by the minute. I could see Mathias's father just down the lane, staring up at us, trying to figure out what was going on. I finally asked the two guards if we could wait a few minutes before we departed—just enough time to let things settle down a bit.

Surprisingly they said no. The *comandante* had told them to return immediately with the merchandise and the thief. That was what they must do.

I came up with an idea. Time spent smoking, I knew from experience, was not real time and not factored into any equation. I told Mathias to offer the two guards cigarettes. They seemed very grateful and lit up immediately. A few minutes went by as they all smoked in silence.

Mathias's father finally departed from his vantage point, apparently reassured that all the commotion was some kind of social visit. I started the van. My passengers extinguished their cigarettes and climbed back in for the trip down the hill to the police station.

Paço Real - Sintra

32

A FEW DAYS LATER BAR-
bara and I were ready to complete the sale of the house. We had
been in touch with one of the English ladies. She and her husband, the barrister, were to arrive Saturday afternoon with the
money and the final transfer documents. We spent all day cleaning the house from top to bottom and placing flowers in strate-
gic locations. We patrolled the pathways for stray chickens and

had even cooked a gourmet meal for the packs of dogs that would keep them in the woods for hours.

After several days of negotiations, I had finally persuaded Comandante Bernardo to relinquish our television and stereo equipment. He had been dead-set on keeping them as evidence for Mathias's trial, a trial that might not take place for several years, if ever, all seemed to agree. In the end I had taken several dozen photos of the television and stereo, both color and black and white, serial numbers included, and a notary came to certify that the photos were indeed of the stolen goods. It was only after all this that we were allowed to bring our property back to Little Cats.

But the excitement of the sale seemed to put the robbery into the background. We were mentally prepared to part with the house, but we didn't think about or discuss the future. We knew only that we wanted to continue to live somewhere in this incredible country that bruised and embraced us at the same time.

We gave the house a few final touches—fresh fruit on the table, a bottle of champagne in the refrigerator—and settled down to await the arrival of the purchasers. An hour passed and then another. The afternoon wore on slowly, punctuated only by visits from several of our neighbors. They had heard the house was for sale. Was there any truth to the rumor?

We tried to explain as best we could—the finances, the unexpected costs. But the villagers' main concern was that we remain among them. Did we need a place to stay after we sold Little Cats? If so, they would arrange one. Uncle Pedro or Aunt Mafalda always had a room available, and we could stay there, of course. It would not do for us to go to another place. We were good people, they said, and brave enough to face the water company.

As we waited, Barbara and I pondered that problem. What should we tell the English couple about the water supply? At present we were using water from two tanks filled with a very long hose running from the architect's house in the upper end of the village. We certainly couldn't expect upper-crust English gentry to thread hose through the village every three to four days. But if we told them there was a problem, the purchase might be jeopardized. The two ladies hadn't asked about water on their previous visit, but then water was taken for granted in more advanced countries.

Just as we were discussing this dilemma, the phone rang. It was the English woman, and she was in tears. She and her husband would not be coming, she said. She was very sorry. They had arrived at the airport, it seemed, but while waiting in line to check in for their flight, they had had a violent altercation. Her husband had punched her and walked off.

Was she all right, I asked, feeling my heart sink.

Yes, she was fine, but her husband seemed to have rather strong reservations about buying a house in Portugal. Perhaps she could convince him later, but for now the sale was off.

Silas and Wheelbarrow

33

A FEW WEEKS LATER WE were destitute. In desperation, Barbara agreed to waitress in a local "gourmet" restaurant. In theory, that might have worked, even with her limited understanding of Portuguese. But in fact it didn't. She constantly misinterpreted orders, bringing finger bowls instead of frappes and sardines instead of sorbets.

I looked for employment, too, and through one of my inquiries landed both a job and a house to live in. There was a very rich American woman who had a large estate just outside the village. She had heard of and seen our renovation of Little Cats and offered me a job as foreman of her small construction crew. She was going away, she said, and needed someone responsible to shepherd her flock of wayward masons and carpenters. I accepted her offer, and Barbara and I were allowed to live in her daughter's house in the village—the very house that we had admired when we first arrived.

We immediately put Little Cats on the rental market, and within a few days a Danish couple appeared. Enamored of the cottage's charm, they signed a six-month rental contract, and we moved up the hill to the house known as Little Chicks, using Barbara's run-away wheelbarrow to cart our worldly, already once-stolen possessions. A quick inspection of Little Chicks, however, left us with the firm conclusion that we might be celebrating a Pyrrhic victory. It was in sad shape. No one had lived there for several months, and it was sorely in need of major repairs. Nevertheless, we were glad to change the contours of our financial landscape. We missed living at Little Cats and enjoying our creation, but we became close friends with the Danish couple and spent many evenings with them in the garden of the cottage under the grape arbor we had constructed.

And as fate would have it, only two weeks later a strange German man showed up in the village unannounced, took one look at the exterior of Little Cats, and said he wanted to buy it. The rental contract was no problem. He had several houses around the world and was in no hurry to occupy the cottage. He gave us a mound of deutsche marks as a deposit and told the agent accompanying him to arrange the paperwork. Then he disappeared.

Meanwhile, at Little Chicks I spent my spare time repairing three-hundred-year-old plumbing and rudimentary electrical systems. Barbara painted, and in the evening we sat on the terrace of the cottage, looking out over the village. It certainly looked better for our efforts, we thought. Our renovation of Little Cats seemed to have motivated other restorations. Already three more abandoned cottages had been purchased and had large crews swarming over them, raising roofs and plastering walls. This was the last authentic village in the Lisbon area, the "last old place," someone had told us, and it now seemed everyone wanted to share the single main road, the little chapel, and even the inconvenient lack of water. Poncho, the famous architect and now our next-door neighbor, summed it up succinctly: "When Salazar was in power," he said, "women's bathing suits had skirts that had to be a certain length. The day Salazar left office, the suits came off completely."

So, Poncho maintained, the same would happen with the countryside. There would be a gradual exodus from the city, a lapse into rusticity. It was chic to be a villager now and commute to Lisbon. Gentrification of the Sintra area was coming again, just as it had hundreds of years ago when the court followed the king like obliging puppies. Poncho himself had started the movement, renovating a humble hovel, spinning a cocoon of scaffolding that, when removed, revealed what he assured us was a new vernacular. The home was a homage to himself and a playful blend of dissident styles, as curvaceous as a well-fed matron and as bright as a tart.

But the dialectics of the house were not important; the structure and Poncho's ebullient personality served to anchor the village. Newcomers would be welcome, we knew, but ultimately the style and the spirit of the place would change. In fact, so attractive was our tiny hamlet becoming that Sandra implored us to let her bring her stable of plutocrats over for several meals. She liked the large, ancient dining room at Little Chicks, she said. And the village, it was so quaint and provincial. The very thing to amuse her guests.

•

AND SO THINGS SLOWLY CAME FULL CIRCLE IN THAT MAGIC IBERIAN way. Barbara was back at her easel, and I was back designing and building things that could only be done here. Another old cottage caught our eye and begged us to dress her up. The villagers were happy that we were still among them and came often to us with their problems, or to share the bounty of their harvest. Mathias, Barbara's ex-student and our personal thief, even managed to escape Comandante Bernardo's clutches. He had enlisted in the army, which automatically sprang him from the local jail.

Thus we enjoyed a few more brief months with our lives approaching the ideal we had envisioned when we first dreamed of moving here. There was only one last piece of unfinished business—the water company. It was still conspicuously absent from the village, as was its service. I decided to give the company bureaucrats one last prod and went to their offices, shovel in hand, accompanied by a Portuguese friend with a camera. We posed for several pictures just outside Conception's office, creating enough commotion so that the people finally came out to see what was going on. Simple, I told them. I was going to start the water project in the village the next day and fully intended to accomplish it alone. The photographer, I said, was from the National Press Services and was going to do an article about me, a crazy foreigner who was determined to take matters into his own hands, tired as he was of waiting for the water company to act.

Would I really do this, they asked.

Oh, yes, I replied. At 8:00 A.M. sharp the following day— unless, of course, they showed up before me and began the project themselves.

They rattled on about the shame it would cause the company if I attempted to do the project alone. They said it was definitely scheduled for next month, and I should be patient.

I told them no.

The following morning I had my coffee at José's bar, then walked down to the base of the village just before 8:00, shovel in hand. I wasn't really sure what I would do next. I thought I might really take a crack at the project, do some things in my spare time, such as run pipe to several of the houses whose families needed running water the most. I began to remove several of the cobblestones carefully, treating them with reverence. But as I set the stones on the wall, I heard the distant rumble of diesel engines. Was it possible? I wasn't sure, but I quickly dug out a few cubic centimeters of earth, then rested my shovel in the hole.

A moment later they arrived—a caravan of supply trucks and earth-moving equipment. Noisily they set themselves up to work as the villagers gathered to witness the miracle, applauding and cheering. One thousand years had passed, and now, it seemed, their fate was finally changing.

A limousine appeared at the end of the convoy and stopped in the middle of the road. A chauffeur opened the door and *Senhor* Soares, the director of the water company, stepped out and walked over to me. He gazed down at the tiny hole I had dug.

"So," he said, "you were really going to do it."

"Yes," I replied. "Of course I was going to do it. But now . . ."

I couldn't think of anything else to say so I just handed him the shovel. He looked at it obliquely, then lifted it into the air. The villagers applauded and cheered.

Soares put the shovel back in the hole and shook my hand. "Do you still want to consult on this project?" he asked.

"Oh, yes," I replied. "Come on up to my office," I said, indicating the bar. "In fact, invite all the men up. There's no sense in rushing the project now. We have all the time in the world."

About the Author

RICHARD HEWITT grew up in the San Francisco Bay area, and has worked as a golf pro, switchboard operator, fireman, and house-builder. Along the way, he has studied at eight universities, including the University of Beirut, Lebanon; the University of Vienna, Austria; and the University of California, Berkeley.

He first visited Portugal in 1971 while writing a novel of absolutely no consequence. Returning to the U.S., he moved to Massachusetts, where he built a Jungian-inspired castle in nearby New York State.

A master builder, Mr. Hewitt also works as a translator in several languages. He and Barbara currently divide their time between the Berkshires of Massachusetts and Sintra, Portugal.